TEACH LIKE FINLAND

TEACH LIKE FINLAND

33 Simple Strategies
for Joyful Classrooms

TIMOTHY D. WALKER

Foreword by Pasi Sahlberg

W. W. NORTON & COMPANY
Independent Publishers Since 1923
NEW YORK   LONDON

For information about permission to reproduce selections from this book, write to Permissions, W. W. Norton & Company, Inc., 500 Fifth Avenue, New York, NY 10110
specialsales@wwnorton.com or 800-233-4830.

For information about special discounts for bulk purchases, please contact W. W. Norton Special Sales at
specialsales@wwnorton.com or 800-233-4830.

Manufacturing by Berryville Graphics
Book design by Molly Heron
Production manager: Christine Critelli

Library of Congress Cataloging-in-Publication Data

Names: Walker, Timothy D., author.
Title: Teach like Finland : 33 simple strategies for joyful classrooms / Timothy D. Walker ; foreword by Pasi Sahlberg.
Description: First Edition. | New York : W.W. Norton & Company, [2017] | Includes bibliographical references and index.
Identifiers: LCCN 2016047589 | ISBN 9781324001256 (hardcover)
Subjects: LCSH: Motivation in education--Finland. | Effective teaching--Finland. | Classroom environment. | Programme for International   Student Assessment.
Classification: LCC LB1065 .W282 2017 | DDC 370.15/4094897--dc23 LC record available at https://lccn.loc.gov/2016047589

A division of W. W. Norton & Company, Inc., 500 Fifth Avenue, New York, NY 10110
www.wwnorton.com

W. W. Norton & Company Ltd., 15 Carlisle Street, London W1D 3BS

ISBN: 978-1-324-00125-6

10 9 8 7 6 5 4 3 2

To my children,
Misaiel Courage
and Adalia Joy

Contents

Acknowledgments   ix

Foreword by Pasi Sahlberg   xi

INTRODUCTION   xxi

1   Well-being   3

   Schedule brain breaks   9

   Learn on the move   15

   Recharge after school   26

   Simplify the space   32

   Breathe fresh air   38

   Get into the wild   42

   Keep the peace   47

2   Belonging   57

   Recruit a welfare team   57

   Know each child   61

   Play with your students   66

   Celebrate their learning   72

   Pursue a class dream   76

   Banish the bullying   82

   Buddy up   86

3 Autonomy 91

    Start with freedom 94

    Leave margin 98

    Offer choices 104

    Plan with your students 108

    Make it real 114

    Demand responsibility 121

4 Mastery 129

    Teach the essentials 130

    Mine the textbook 137

    Leverage the tech 141

    Bring in the music 145

    Coach more 150

    Prove the learning 157

    Discuss the grades 163

5 Mind-set 167

    Seek flow 170

    Have a thicker skin 174

    Collaborate over coffee 178

    Welcome the experts 182

    Vacate on vacation 185

    Don't forget joy 188

REFERENCES 191

INDEX 199

Acknowledgments

ABOUT THREE YEARS AGO, I RECEIVED A BRIEF EMAIL from an editor named Deborah in New York City. (I was halfway through my first year of teaching in Helsinki and I was running a little blog called *Taught by Finland.*) Deborah wanted to know if I'd thought of writing a book. I hadn't.

I'm so grateful to Deborah Malmud for believing, from the very beginning, that I could write *Teach Like Finland.* Also, I'm thankful for the rest of the Norton team for their world-class assistance throughout this project.

Additionally, I want to thank Pasi Sahlberg who, since my first year of teaching in Helsinki, has encouraged me to keep writing about Finnish education from an outsider's perspective; I'm so glad he wrote this book's foreword. Also, I'm grateful for my former colleagues and students at Ressu Comprehensive School, where I worked for two good years. In writing this book, I chatted with a handful of Finnish educators from other schools, and I'm thankful for their willingness to speak with me.

Before teaching in Helsinki, I was mentored by several gifted American educators. Many thanks to Brian, Henry, Joanna, Kathy, Linda Lue, Lisa, Steven, and Tricia. Additionally, I want to express my gratitude for my wife Johanna and our children Misaiel and Adalia, whose love brings me a lot of joy. And lastly, I give my deepest thanks to God for his gracious provision.

Foreword

—Pasi Sahlberg

IN THE YEAR 2000, A BOOK LIKE THIS COULD NOT have been written. Back then the global education landscape looked very different. England had just seen a decade full of fundamental school reforms that highlighted higher attainment targets and frequent student assessments, shaking up the lives of all students and teachers. Sweden was in the midst of implementing one of the most radical school reforms, with vouchers that created new types of free schools for parents who were keen to choose alternative education for their children. South East Asia, Japan, Hong Kong, South Korea and Singapore were tuning up their education systems for a faster pace and higher learning outcomes, especially in reading, mathematics, and science (Hargreaves and Shirley, 2010). The United States was running experiments in many of its states that focused on tightening accountability for teachers and schools in search of gains in student achievement and graduation rates. That time was the beginning of an era of increasing effort for higher achievement. If this book had ever been written in 2000 it would have, just like many similar books at that time, advocated for new models of teacher effectiveness, strategies to turn around failing schools, or imperatives to fix entire education systems.

If you'd asked at an international education gathering where the participants would travel to look for inspiration and good ideas for their own work in educational development or school improvement, most would have probably chosen the countries mentioned above. You would have also heard some of them mention what was happening in Australia, New Zealand, Germany, or the Netherlands. Some of these education systems had implemented new, interesting models of monitoring educational progress, informing parents about how well schools were doing, and creating new forms of educational leadership. Study tour destinations and joint research projects that investigated innovation and change regularly included many of these same countries. There was one country that only a very few would have pointed out as having anything interesting to offer when it came to education: Finland.

Everything changed overnight in December 2001. When the Organization for Economic Cooperation and Development (OECD) made public the result of its first international study on what 15-year-olds can do with reading, mathematical, and scientific skills they have acquired in and out of schools, known as PISA (Programme for International Student Assessment), all eyes turned to the tiny Nordic country (OECD, 2001). Against all odds, Finland, with a population of barely 5.5 million people, had scored above all other 31 OECD countries in this test that was supposed to indicate how well young people would succeed in dynamic knowledge economies in adulthood. Furthermore, it appeared that in Finland there was little variation in student achievement between schools, and that children's learning in school was influenced less by family background than in other countries. On top of all this, Finns seemed to have accomplished these admirable results with only modest spending in their schools. No wonder the world of education was confused.

The international education community and global media outlets were not the only ones puzzled by Finland's unexpected center court position. There was also quite a bit of turbulence among education authorities, academics, and pundits in Finland itself. Nobody seemed to have a good enough explanation for the superior educational performance of Finnish schools by international standards. All the way until December 2001, Finland's 9-year comprehensive school (grade one to grade nine) that was launched in the 1970s received increasingly fierce criticism from various fronts in Finnish society. High schools and universities were accusing this new school for slowly but surely declining the level of knowledge and skills that students were expected to possess at the entry to further studies. Some employers joined the choir, adding that the younger generation lacked a good work ethic and were often taught to seek comfort and avoid hard work. Then there were the parents who thought that children who were more able and talented didn't have enough room in the comprehensive school to bloom into their full potentials. Solutions, when offered, included imitating what the rest of the world was doing.

The menu of suggested reforms included creating higher standards, having more detailed information about students' achievement, giving parents more choice regarding where to send their children to school, and creating specialized schools for gifted students. Much of this resistance to Finland's comprehensive school was muted after December 2001. It is fair to bet that without PISA, this book would probably never been written.

How have the Finns responded to thousands of questions and inquires about the success of their schools? Many Finns believe that there are five critical elements that allow Finnish students to fare better than most of their peers in other countries. Four of them are directly associated with schools and their mandates, one is about what happens when children are not in school. You should, however, keep in mind that explaining why something happens in complex social systems always includes a reasonable amount of speculation, and can never be 100 percent certain.

First, we argue that the comprehensive school that children start when they turn seven provides balanced, holistic, and child-focused education and development to all children, and lays a foundation for good, equitable learning. The curriculum in Finnish schools addresses all subjects evenly and thereby provides all children with opportunities to cultivate multiple aspects of their personalities and talents. The absence of private schools and the between-school competition that often comes with them means that all schools must be good schools—regardless of where they are and who they serve. The majority of Finnish pupils study in socially mixed classes without being tracked or segregated by their ability or socio-economic status. During the past four decades now, this spirit of inclusiveness has shaped the mind-sets of teachers and parents alike to believe that anyone can learn most of the expected things in school as long as there is appropriate and sufficient support. As a result, focus on children's well-being, health, and happiness in school has become one of the key goals of schooling across the country.

Second, we realized early on that successfully teaching heterogeneous classes would require better-trained teachers than what we had had until the 1970s. As a result, teacher education was shifted from colleges to research universities. As part of the comprehensive higher education reform in the 1980s, teachers also had to graduate from research-based masters degree programs just like any other professional in Finland. Newly-graduated teachers had therefore studied much more child psychology, pedagogy, special education, subject didactics, and curriculum than their more-seasoned colleagues, which equipped them with broader professional responsibilities in their schools. In the 1990s teachers were expected to collectively design their school curricula, choose the most effective ways to teach, assess how well their students had learned, and self-direct their own professional development and growth as teachers. Continuous strengthening of the teaching profession in Finland has built strong and notable trust in teachers and schools that, in turn, has further enhanced the status of teachers and attractiveness of becoming a teacher among young Finns.

Third, we decided to establish permanent mechanisms to secure and enhance children's well-being and health in all schools. The main goal was to ensure that lack of basic health and care at home would not jeopardize pupils' chances to succeed. The backbone of this support system was a new special education structure that assumed that problems related to education should be identified and addressed as early as possible. Each school is given sufficient resources and personnel to accomplish this. Every school in Finland has to establish a Student Welfare Team that consists of experts, teachers, and leadership who discuss concerning issues and decide how to tackle them in the best possible ways. Needless to say, having all these special education services up and running in all schools requires that funding be designed in such a way that schools with more special educational needs also are allocated more funds. This has created an essential basis for strong, system-wide educational equity in Finland.

Fourth, we think that mid-level educational leadership, i.e. schools and local districts, should be in the hands of experienced and qualified educators. Indeed, we expect that the school principal be qualified to teach in the school that she leads. School leaders must also be suitable and fit to lead people and learning organizations. Leadership hierarchy in Finnish schools is relatively flat; most principals also teach students alongside their leadership tasks. This guarantees that leaders in schools also have direct links to classroom experience. We have noted that teachers are often more likely to accept feedback and talk about their concerns when they know that their bosses also teach and may face similar questions in their classrooms. I have argued (Sahlberg, 2015) that in Finnish schools, leaders are teachers and teachers are (pedagogical) leaders.

Fifth, we know that students' out-of-school situations

explain a significant part of the variation in their in-school learning. Although in Finland family background, for example, has weaker association with students' achievement than in many other countries, what happens to young people when they are not in school has an important role to play in both educational success and failure. Therefore, particular child and youth policies together with a dense network of associations, clubs, and organizations have a significant positive impact on children's well-being, health, and social capital, which all contribute to their learning in school. There are about 100,000 nongovernmental associations with some 15 million members in Finland (Allianssi, 2016). This suggests that Finns are actively taking part in various activities outside their work or school. Three out of five young Finns are engaged in some type of social activity in their free time. The most common of these associations offer activities in sports, arts and culture. In these organizations, young people learn complementary knowledge and skills to those they also learn in schools. When 90 percent of young Finns report that they have at least one hobby outside school, this obviously has a role to play in how they do in school as well. Universal early childhood development and care, public healthcare, and a dense public library system are among those factors that support the work of schools in helping all children to succeed.

It is difficult to understand how education systems work, and how different elements within and outside of them affect outcomes. It is therefore very difficult to make good sense of education systems other than the one you have been part of yourself. A weeklong visit to observe schools and listen to experts rarely provides enough insight to understand what

Finland's education is really about. What you need instead is to become a teacher in Finland—to be taught by Finland. This is what makes Tim Walker a unique messenger in the world of educational improvement. His writings reflect a broader understanding of the fine cultural fabric of Finnish schools, and are illuminating for both foreign and Finland based educators.

I met Tim soon after he had moved with his family from Boston to Helsinki. We had several conversations back then about how Finnish schools differ from typical American schools. I was fascinated to listen to his stories about his fifth grade classroom. During his time at Ressu Comprehensive School—a Helsinki public school, which also offers International Baccalaureate programs, a place I have visited often and know well—Tim was confronted with many of the ingredients of Finnish schools that you can read in a fully matured format in this book. Writing about these important practical aspects of what makes Finland's schools different requires an alien's perspective. I can't think of anybody who could do this better than Tim.

When I was about to publish the second edition of my book *Finnish Lessons: What Can the World Learn from Educational Change in Finland*, I asked if my publisher would paste a sticker on the back cover saying something like "WARNING: Don't try this at home." The reason for this was the huge number of inquiries from politicians, education leaders, and teachers asking how to implement the Finnish school system in their own countries. My publisher understood my concern, but they didn't allow a sticker. Nevertheless, I think it is impossible to transfer education systems from one place to another. Education systems are complex cultural, organic entities like plants or trees that grow well only in their home soil and climate. Tim Walker's book *Teach Like Finland: 33 Simple Strategies for Joyful Classrooms* makes this clear and instead offers you some practical steps about how to incorporate more happiness and enjoyment in schools. If you are able to do that with the ideas that follow, then you'll be teaching a bit like Finland. Good luck!

References

Allianssi (2016). *Nuorista Suomessa*. Helsinki: Allianssi.

Hargreaves, A. and Shirley, D. (2012). *The Global Fourth Way. The quest for educational excellence.* Thousand Oaks: Corwin.

OECD (2001). *Knowledge and Skills for Life. First results from PISA 2000.* Paris: OECD.

Sahlberg, P. (2015). *Finnish Lessons 2.0: What can the world learn from educational change in Finland.* New York: Teachers College Press.

Introduction

IN MY FIRST YEAR AS A CLASSROOM TEACHER IN ARLING-
ton, Massachusetts, I was on the fast track to burnout. On
weekdays I would arrive at my school around 6:30 A.M.
and exit sometime in the evening, usually with a backpack
full of teaching guides. When I wasn't at school, I tried
disconnecting from the work, but I couldn't. At breakfast
I anxiously pored over my lesson plans, and in the evening, as I lay in bed I obsessed about all of the things I
was doing "wrong." On a typical night I'd wake up four or
five times. Sometimes I felt so anxious in the morning that
I'd run to the bathroom in my apartment and throw up—
gross, I know.

Before starting this first year of classroom teaching, I
was so enthusiastic, so confident that I'd *love* this job. But
when October arrived, I started to admit to myself that I
was *hating* this job. It wasn't bringing me joy. The opposite
was taking place, actually.

My Finnish wife, Johanna, was very worried about me.

She warned that if I didn't slow down I'd need to take a leave of absence. I said, "Never." Johanna wondered why I insisted on working nonstop. She told me about her Finnish friend in Helsinki, a first grade teacher just like me, who worked no more than six hours every day, including an hour or two of prep. When she left her public school around 2:00 P.M., she left all of her work behind, too.

I assumed that Johanna misunderstood her friend's workload. Or, I reasoned, if my wife had the facts straight, her friend wasn't a good teacher. Good teachers, I told my wife, don't do short workdays. In fact, I explained, they push themselves—to the limit.

"Not in Finland," Johanna said.

After my wife graduated from Finnish high school, she spent a few months working as a substitute teacher in Helsinki, which provided her with a behind-the-scenes look at the working lives of Finland's educators. In Finnish schools, teachers and students typically have a fifteen-minute break built into every hour of class, and, in Johanna's experience, most educators would spend their breaks in the lounge—drinking coffee, chatting with colleagues, and flipping through magazines. It sounded, given my American teaching experience, pretty farfetched.

At my Massachusetts school, during my extended lunch block—usually my only scheduled break during my workday—I'd often work through the free time, zigzagging across my American classroom with a peeled banana, nibbling on-the-go as I prepped for afternoon lessons.

Throughout my first year of classroom teaching, my Finnish wife was doing her best to convince me that there was another way to teach. And not just survive but thrive. I wasn't buying it, though.

My reality, which I shared with many American teachers, seemed too different from those teachers in Finland. I didn't have those fifteen-minute breaks scattered throughout the day. My last class was still in session when Johanna's friend would leave her school at 2 P.M. And I had, from my perspective, a mountain of classroom prep waiting for me after I waved goodbye to my first graders around 3:00 P.M.

During my rookie year of classroom teaching, I was typically putting in twelve-hour days, and somehow I thought this made me a much better teacher than Johanna's friend. But by the end of that year, I knew I was clearly the weaker educator. A terrible lack of work–life balance had caught up to me, and I was brimming over with stress and anxiety. Worst of all, the job of teaching was no longer joyful, and my lack of satisfaction seemed to be rubbing off on my students. Those little kids often looked miserable, too.

That school year, I remember a veteran colleague telling me that 50 percent of American teachers leave the profession within five years. And I thought I was going to be one of those early dropouts. In late February, my anxiety and level of sleep deprivation had become so intense that I could no longer prepare lessons for the next day of school. I remember having sessions at my desk, where I'd spend minutes staring blankly at my planner. One late afternoon, after another fruitless hour of classroom prep, I returned home and collapsed on the kitchen floor, lying speechless on the ground while my wife pleaded that I take a break. Humbly, after weeks of sleepless nights, I picked up the phone and requested a leave of absence.

I felt ready to move on from the profession and pretend that it had just been a bad dream. But I also wondered if my Finnish wife was right.

Was it possible to teach *and* thrive? Even in an American classroom?

Three years later, Johanna and I decided to move to Finland. It wasn't because I wanted to flee American education. On the contrary: I didn't want to leave. I was still teaching at the same school, grateful to have survived that embarrassing first year. After my month-long leave of absence, I had received valuable support and experience, and, over time, I was starting to tap into the joys of teaching, despite feeling physically and emotionally exhausted when I returned home from school every day.

The year before we moved to Helsinki, I was teaching full-time, completing graduate coursework, and working several part-time jobs. All things considered, I wasn't spending nearly as much time at home as I would have wished— and maybe, if I was honest with myself, I was slowly starting to burn out again. We decided to move to Finland, where we hoped for a slower pace, especially during our children's early years. (Today we have two children under five years old.)

When I announced our plan to settle in Helsinki, my American principal remarked that it was a career move for me. I remember laughing at the idea, because it felt like the opposite. I was prepared, in Finland, to stop teaching all together, just to live a more balanced life. We purchased our one-way tickets to Helsinki without knowing if I would even have a job.

In late June 2013, one month before moving overseas, I still lacked a job as a classroom teacher, but I received a curious e-mail one morning from a Helsinki principal. I had contacted her in March, along with several other Finnish principals, and when I hadn't heard from any of them, I had stopped hoping. But there in my inbox that June morning was this message, which invited me to chat about the possibility of teaching an English-speaking fifth grade class at a Helsinki public school. My jaw dropped.

Later that week over Skype the Finnish principal interviewed me, and at the end of the conversation she offered me the position. I was over the moon, and I gratefully accepted the job. But then I began to worry: what was I signing up for exactly?

I heard, like so many Americans, that Finnish education was top-notch. But, in practice, what did that mean? Johanna had already told me bits of information about Finnish schools—the short days and the fifteen-minute breaks, mostly. And in one education documentary, I learned that Finland's fifteen-year-olds consistently performed well on a set of international tests called the PISA (Programme for International Student Assessment), which measures critical-thinking skills in the areas of reading, math, and science. All told, I knew very little about Finnish education when I signed up for that fifth grade teaching job in Helsinki.

Regardless, I was embarking on a two-year journey to see Finland's school system from the inside. It was an uncertain destination, where I expected to struggle to assimilate. And I confess that I would struggle, but not necessarily in the ways that my fellow American teachers might expect.

Typically, a person who moves from one country to

another experiences culture shock, the phenomenon of feeling lost in an unfamiliar environment. But for me, given that my wife is Finnish and I had visited her home country about a dozen times before moving, I mostly avoided culture shock, except for one area of my life: the workplace.

My Helsinki school felt like a foreign land, a place where I'd find new expectations and new rules to follow, and in that very different context, I found myself rethinking the "best practices" I had learned in American schools. Over those two years in Helsinki, I received many opportunities to study Finland's teaching practices up close, observing my colleagues for more than one hundred classroom hours and completing my teaching practicum, supervised by two veteran Finnish colleagues, for my American master's degree in elementary education.

In writing this book, I was curious to see if other teachers in Finland were employing similar practices I had witnessed in Helsinki, so I visited several schools around Finland. Also, I interviewed Finnish teachers at the preschool, primary, and secondary levels. In doing so, I learned that many of the teaching practices I saw in Helsinki could be found throughout Finland.

The strategies I found weren't flashy like 1:1 iPad implementation, nor did they seem idealistically abstract like, "Just trust the students, ya'll!" The teaching methods were simple, effective practices that could benefit *any* classroom. And, best of all, I found that many of the strategies, when I implemented them, brought joy to my classroom. Probably these Finnish practices would need to be adapted slightly to work in another teaching context, like America's, but they certainly weren't "Finland-only" methods.

Consider, for example, one of the strategies I suggest in this book: taking little brain breaks throughout the school day. Without educational policy change, American teachers would find it difficult to implement the frequent Finnish-style fifteen-minute breaks of free play, but it's not too difficult to imagine that U.S. teachers could teach *like* Finland by offering their students tiny chunks of "choice time" throughout the day, in an effort to keep kids fresh and focused in the classroom.

In this book, I'm interested in looking at what American teachers—inspired by Finland's education approach—can do *today* that will make a positive difference in their classrooms, despite the obvious systemic differences described by Pasi Sahlberg in the foreword.

When the first PISA results were announced in 2001, Finland was shocked to find itself ranked number one as an education system. Its softer approach of short schools days, light homework loads, and little standardized testing bucked the conventional wisdom of how to get great learning outcomes. This tiny Nordic country was suggesting to America, and the rest of the world, that there is another way to do school, without narrowing the curriculum and stressing out teachers and kids. That different methodology is evident at the policy level, but it's also observed on the microscale, in Finnish classrooms.

As American teachers, Finnish educators will probably not inspire us with innovative teaching strategies, because many of Finland's pedagogical innovations have been adopted from North America and elsewhere (Sahlberg, 2015). But what we can learn from teachers in Finland, based on what I've experienced, is the way in which they seem to value happiness more than achievement. They make small, simple decisions to promote joyful teaching and learning, and in the end, as numerous PISA tests have shown, their students do well anyway.

Like many American teachers, I read Doug Lemov's book *Teach Like a Champion 2.0* and discovered a collection of helpful classroom strategies. But there was one strategy I found puzzling: "Joy Factor." Joy in the classroom, suggests Lemov (2015), is a tool that a teacher can leverage to raise achievement:

> Of course, Joy Factor moments are not ends in themselves. Good Joy Factor in the classroom has to be "the servant"—that is, its purpose is to support the day's objective. It should also be something you can quickly turn on and off. (p. 442)

While Lemov appears to view joy as a strategy, I'm proposing that we start to see prioritizing joy (or happiness), inspired by the Finnish approach to education, as an overarching goal in our classrooms. Happiness can be understood as "a state of heightened positive emotion" and instead of sidetracking the teaching and learning in our classrooms, it can improve productivity and enhance social and emotional intelligence (Seppälä, 2016, p. 8).

I understand that prioritizing happiness in our classrooms may seem like an abstract idea. Here's one way of thinking about it: when we're seeking to sleep better, we prioritize it by taking different steps before we crawl into bed, such as exercising and powering off our cell phones (Raghunathan, 2016). Similarly, we can put joy first in our classrooms by using a collection of strategies.

During my years of working and living in Finland, I have identified a handful of steps that educators can take to promote joyful teaching and learning. Raj Raghunathan, professor at the McCombs School at the University of Texas at Austin and the author of *If You're So Smart, Why Aren't You Happy?* (2016), recognizes four ingredients of happiness (if basic needs like food and shelter have been addressed): belonging, autonomy, mastery, and mind-set (Pinsker, 2016). One ingredient that I've added to this list is well-being, which I view as foundational in order to develop the other components. I've organized *Teach Like Finland*'s thirty-three simple strategies around these five ingredients of happiness, applying them to the context of a joyful classroom.

TEACH LIKE FINLAND

Well-being

WE MOVED TO HELSINKI IN LATE JULY, AND BEFORE
school began IN mid-August my family and I spent several evenings strolling though our new city. In every
park I remember visiting, I saw an unfamiliar sight:
dozens of locals doing nothing but sitting on blankets,
drinking wine, and chatting. They weren't in a rush, it
seemed, to get anything done. They were simply enjoying those warm, sunny evenings with their close friends.

Life in Finland seemed much slower than the pace of
life I had experienced in America. And I confess that,
after living in high-powered Boston, I was initially
attracted to the relaxed atmosphere in Helsinki—but I
remained skeptical of this approach to life. What were

these folks ultimately achieving, I wondered, by simply lounging around for hours on those blankets?

Despite burning out during my first year of teaching, I was still clinging to this ideology—years later in Helsinki—that my worth could be quantified by my productivity. "Tim, you're not a human *doing*," a mentor teacher in Boston used to remind me. "You're a human *being*." Even in Finland, those were words I still needed to hear.

I think the slower pace of this tiny Nordic country eventually rubbed off on me, because during those first weeks of teaching in Helsinki I tried to be more intentional about working less after school. When I returned home in the late afternoon, I left my schoolwork in my backpack (something that didn't feel natural, initially) so I could focus on playing with my one-year-old and catching up with my wife.

In Helsinki I was starting to feel more like a human *being*, but I confess that it was a different story at school. Initially I wasn't prepared to adopt a different approach to my work as a teacher. And my Finnish colleagues were starting to notice.

Just as my wife had told me, at my Helsinki school I found frequent fifteen-minute breaks throughout each day, and typically my colleagues were spending many of these breaks in the teachers' lounge. (During breaks, several teachers took turns supervising the younger students outdoors and the older students indoors.) But even after three weeks of school, I still hadn't spent two free minutes in the lounge taking a break with my colleagues. I'd only quickly enter that space to fetch my mail every morning, and then I'd make a beeline to my classroom.

In those brief moments of entering the lounge, I saw something similar to what I discovered while strolling through parks in downtown Helsinki. Many of my colleagues were sipping coffee, flipping through newspapers, and chatting leisurely with one another. And, oftentimes, when I walked by the lounge, I heard them laughing loudly. I was starting to suspect that my colleagues were lazy.

In September, over the course of a week, three of my Finnish colleagues told me that they worried I might burn out, because they hadn't seen me in the teachers' lounge. I admitted to them that I was spending all of those fifteen-minute breaks in my classroom, working hard on different teaching-related tasks. These three colleagues suggested that I change my routine.

At first I laughed off their concern. I told them I knew what it was like to burn out, and I assured them that I was doing just fine. But they remained steadfast: they were serious about the importance of taking little breathers throughout the day. One of my colleagues told me that she *needed* to spend a few minutes every day in the lounge, slowing down with other teachers. She claimed it made her a better teacher.

At the time I felt so confused because my impulse to work nonstop—often sacrificing my well-being in the short term—didn't seem like something that many of my Finnish colleagues supported. I had always believed that the best educators were the ones who worked the hardest, even if it meant surviving on a few hours of sleep, skipping lunch breaks in exchange for more time for lesson prep, and never finding any time to socialize with colleagues. Many of the teachers I had most admired in the United States were brimming with passion for their profession, just like me, but always seemed to be on the brink of burning out. But in

Helsinki I didn't see my Finnish colleagues working through lunch breaks or hiding in their classrooms for the entirety of each day. Almost always, they looked relatively stress-free compared with what I had seen in American schools. And, unsurprisingly, their students did, too.

I've heard several critics of the Finnish education model suggest that one major reason the United States can't learn from this tiny Nordic country is cultural differences. But I think this *is* one area where we can learn from Finland's schools. As Americans, our cultural priorities—which seem to say, ultimately, that chasing success (or "being the best") is what matters most in life—greatly diminish our well-being and, consequentially, the well-being of our nation's children.

The push for America's kids to succeed starts, for many of them, as babies. This is especially evident among wealthy families. Parents purchase flash cards and educational games, and for toddlers they scout out the best pre-schools, institutions that may cost more than $30,000 a year, to give their kids an early academic edge. Scores of American parents decline to send their children to kindergarten, a concept researchers call redshirting, so that their kids will be a year older and more developmentally advanced, which would translate, hypothetically, into better academic performance. During the middle school years some parents slap bumper stickers on their cars that read "Proud parent of an honor roll student." In high school, many students are advised to pad their resumes if they want to get into the best colleges, so they stretch themselves thin by maintaining high GPAs, loading up on extracurricular activities, taking AP classes, and signing up for private SAT tutoring. This pressure to excel in high school varies across the country, but in some places, like Palo Alto, California, suicide rates among high school students are staggeringly high.

Emma Seppälä, a researcher at Stanford University and the author of *The Happiness Track* (2016), recalled her early experiences as an intern working for a large newspaper in Paris, France. In the early morning hours, she would make trips between the second floor and the basement transporting memos and other items. On the second floor Seppälä observed many American writers in cubicles, while in the basement she found working-class French press workers:

> On the second floor, you could feel the tension in the air. The floor was quiet except for the sounds of typing and printing. The editors—most of them overweight with dark circles under their eyes—were huddled over their screens, keeping to themselves and eating pizza at their desks. But in the basement, the mood was downright festive. French wine, cheese, and bread were all laid out on a huge table ... Soon, I found myself wishing for more reasons to join that joyful atmosphere.
>
> Working at the newspaper, going back and forth between these two groups got me thinking: Here was a team of people—editors, writers, and press workers—working through the night to finish and distribute a newspaper by dawn. Yes, it's true that the two groups performed different tasks and came from different cultures—but they were both working to meet the same urgent deadline ... Night after night, despite the challenges, both groups successfully completed

their jobs. Yet they went about it in opposite ways: one group was stressed, burned out, and unhealthy looking; the other happy, energetic, and thriving. (p. 1)

When I first read this passage in *The Happiness Track*, I immediately thought of how closely Seppälä's description of the newspaper's second floor mirrored my experiences within American schools and how her portrait of the printing room paralleled my experiences within Finnish schools. Like the American writers and the French workers, teachers in America and teachers in Finland are working to meet a similar deadline—to get kids to learn every hour, every day, every year. But, in my experience, the process in which that deadline is met typically looks quite different in these two countries: one teaching approach seems faster, harder, and more achievement focused, while the other seems slower, softer, and more well-being focused.

"Decades of research have shown that happiness is not the *outcome* of success but rather its *precursor*," writes Seppälä. "In other words, if you want to succeed, you have to be more like the French press workers in the basement" (2016, p. 7).

The foundation for experiencing happiness is having our basic needs met, so adequate sleep, food, water, clothing, and shelter are prerequisites for ourselves and the students in our classrooms. In developed nations, like the United States and Finland, teachers are not generally tasked with caring for children who enter school with unmet basic needs. That said, more than 16 million U.S. children—about 22 percent of the overall population—come from families with incomes below America's federal poverty level, according to the National Center for Children in Poverty (2016), and I recognize, sadly, that a significant portion of America's student population experience food insecurity or even homelessness. This situation, where children enter classrooms with unmet basic needs, is uniquely challenging, and I'm not in a position to offer advice. What I can suggest, though, are several strategies I've learned in Finnish schools that promote the physical, emotional, and mental health of teachers and students. And these simple steps, ultimately, improve the quality of teaching and learning and make our classrooms more joyful.

Schedule brain breaks

Like a zombie, Sami*—one of my fifth graders—lumbered over to me and hissed, "I think I'm going to explode! I'm not used to this schedule." And I believed him. An angry red rash was starting to form on his forehead.

Yikes, I thought, *what a way to begin my first year of teaching in Finland.* It was only the third day of school, and I was already pushing a student to the breaking point. When I took him aside, I quickly discovered why he was so upset.

Throughout this first week of school, I had gotten creative with my fifth grade timetable. If you recall, students in Finland normally take a fifteen-minute break for every forty-five minutes of instruction. During a typical break, the children head outside to play and socialize with friends.

I didn't see the point of these frequent pit stops. As a teacher in the United States, I'd usually spent consecutive hours with my students in the classroom. And I was trying to replicate this model in Finland. The Finnish way seemed soft, and I was convinced that kids learned better with lon-

---

* The names used for students in this book are pseudonyms.

ger stretches of instructional time. So I decided to hold my students back from their regularly scheduled break and teach two forty-five-minute lessons in a row, followed by a double break of thirty minutes. Now I knew why the red dots had appeared on Sami's forehead.

Come to think of it, I wasn't sure if the American approach had ever worked very well. My students in the States had always seemed to drag their feet after about forty-five minutes in the classroom. But they'd never thought of revolting like this shrimpy Finnish fifth grader, who was digging in his heels on the third day of school. At that moment, I decided to embrace the Finnish model of taking breaks.

Once I incorporated these short recesses into our timetable, I no longer saw feet-dragging, zombie-like kids in my classroom. Throughout the school year, my Finnish students would, without fail, enter the classroom with a bounce in their steps after a fifteen-minute break. And most important, they were more focused during lessons.

At first I was convinced that I had made a groundbreaking discovery: frequent breaks kept students fresh throughout the day. But then I remembered that Finns have known this for years—they've been providing breaks to their students since the 1960s.

In my quest to understand the value of the Finnish practice, I stumbled upon the work of Anthony Pellegrini, author of the book *Recess: Its Role in Education and Development* and emeritus professor of educational psychology at the University of Minnesota—who has praised this approach for more than a decade. In East Asia, where many primary schools provide their students with a ten-minute break after about forty minutes of classroom instruction, Pellegrini observed the same phenomenon that I had witnessed at my Finnish school. After these shorter recesses, students appeared to be more focused in the classroom (Pellegrini, 2005).

Not satisfied with anecdotal evidence alone, Pellegrini and his colleagues ran a series of experiments at a U.S. public elementary school to explore the relationship between recess timing and attentiveness in the classroom. In every one of the experiments, students were more attentive after a break than before a break. They also found that the children were less focused when the timing of the break was delayed—or in other words, when the lesson dragged on (Pellegrini, 2005).

In Finland, primary school teachers seem to know this intuitively. They send kids outside—rain or shine—for their frequent recesses. And the children get to decide how they spend their break times.

Although I favor the Finnish model, I realize that unleashing fifth graders on the playground every hour would be a huge shift for most schools. According to Pellegrini, breaks don't have to be held outdoors to be beneficial. In one of his experiments at a public elementary school, the children had their recess times inside the school, and the results matched those of other experiments where they took their breaks outside: after their breaks, the students were more focused in class (Pellegrini, 2005).

What I realized in Finland, with the help of a flustered fifth grader, is that once I started to see a break as a strategy to maximize learning, I stopped feeling guilty about shortening classroom instruction. Pellegrini's findings confirm that frequent breaks boost attentiveness in class. With this in mind, we no longer need to fear that students won't learn what they need to learn if we let them disconnect from their work several times throughout the school day.

. . .

THE YEAR BEFORE I ARRIVED IN HELSINKI, THE AMERican researcher and kinesiologist Debbie Rhea visited Finnish schools, and she, too, was inspired by their frequent fifteen-minute breaks. When she returned to the States, she piloted a study to evaluate the learning benefits of a Finland-inspired schedule with multiple recesses throughout the school day (Turner, 2013).

Today, Rhea's research project is up and running in a handful of American schools in several states, and so far the early results have been promising. Educators at Eagle Mountain Elementary School in Fort Worth, Texas, report a significant change in their students, who receive four fifteen-minute breaks each day; for example, they are more focused, and they are not tattling as often. One first grade teacher even noticed that her students are no longer chewing on pencils (Connelly, 2016).

Rhea's research is exciting, and it seems like the national interest in bringing more breaks to American schools is high. However, while the tide might be changing in American education, many U.S. teachers and students lack the freedom to imitate the Finnish model. Thankfully, any classroom, even non-Finnish ones, can tap into the benefits of taking multiple breaks throughout each day.

Initially, I thought that the true value of Finnish-style breaks is related to free play, but I no longer hold this view. I've concluded that the primary benefit of Finnish breaks is in the way it keeps kids focused by refreshing their brains. Daniel Levitin, professor of psychology, behavioral neuroscience, and music at McGill University, believes that giving the brain time to rest, through regular breaks, leads to greater productivity and creativity. "You need to give your brain time to consolidate all the information that's come in," he said in an interview for the education blog *MindShift* (Schwartz, 2014). But even without scheduled breaks at school, the mind rests naturally through daydreaming, which "allows you to refresh and release all those neural circuits that get all bound up when you're focused," said Levitin. "Children shouldn't be overly scheduled. They should have blocks of time to promote spontaneity and creativity" (Schwartz, 2014).

There are different ways of offering little brain breaks, which I describe below, but one of the most important things to remember is that they need to happen regularly to benefit our students. In other words, it's wise to schedule them throughout the day. A good start, perhaps, would be thinking about offering a whole-group brain break for every forty-five minutes of classroom instruction—just like many Finnish teachers. But even that timing could be too infrequent for your students. What's important is that you watch your students carefully. If they seem to be dragging their feet before the forty-five-minute mark, it would seem beneficial to offer a brain break right away.

In her book *Overwhelmed* (2014), journalist Brigid Schulte dives into the subject of overworking and the struggle to maintain a healthy work–life balance. Throughout the book, Schulte suggests different strategies for promoting well-being. One of her favorite methods is something she describes as pulsing, switching between work and rest. Pulsing is based on this idea that when we spend all our time working, our bodies break the natural rhythm they thrive upon, in which we alternate between work and rest.

Pulsing looks different in different contexts. Schulte lauds the importance of taking regular breaks throughout the workday (a la Finnish school style). With her own work as a journalist, she aims to write for several 1.5-hour-long bursts throughout the day, in which she stays off her phone and e-mail (Schulte, 2014).

What would pulsing look like in the classroom? I think it's as simple as providing students with predictable breaks between long stretches of classroom instruction. I don't think these breaks need to be free play, as they are in Finland. Teachers can offer several blocks of *choice time* throughout the day, in which their students can select from a range of options, ten minutes of free reading, free writing, or playing a fun math game, for example.

In my opinion, there are three qualities that choice time should possess: a high degree of enjoyment, independence, and novelty. Forcing everyone to read silently for ten minutes isn't a break, especially when your students have been engaged in a reader's workshop for the last hour. But I believe that providing everyone with a few engaging options after a reader's workshop can refresh children and serve as a good bridge to the next lesson, whatever that may be.

These built-in breaks are especially important for elementary school classrooms, where students and teachers typically spend consecutive hours with one another. For middle school and high school teachers, scheduling breaks may not be as vital, because their students may spend only forty-five to fifty minutes in their classrooms on a daily basis, with a few minutes of unstructured time between classes. (Instead, what may serve as valuable for secondary school teachers is a mindfulness exercise to start or end each lesson; see "Keep the peace," below.)

Some students, I've found, need breaks more often than their peers. One way to accommodate these students is by offering an area in the classroom where students can take a break. One researcher, Amanda Moreno, has noted the value of something called a "calm spot." Teachers have told Moreno that, thanks to calm spots, some of their students who once had several tantrums per day now have zero (Deruy, 2016).

It's wise to talk with your students about how you're on a mission to help them learn better by inserting predictable breaks into the school day, and how you'd like their feedback in crafting an ideal choice time (with independent activities they find novel and enjoyable). This gesture not only will promote shared ownership of student learning but also will likely produce valuable insight.

Learn on the move

"Psst. Can I speak with you for a second?" My sharp-eyed mentor teacher in Arlington, Massachusetts, pulled me aside during a lunch break. She wasn't wearing her characteristic smile. "Tim, please don't be offended by what I'm about to say," she said, "but whenever I peek into your classroom, you always seem to be sitting down with your first graders on the rug." The criticism stung—not because it was off-target, but because I knew it was true.

My habit of requiring my young students to sit passively for a half-hour or so on the rug was clearly not working for them. By the time I'd release them from the rug to do independent work, they were exasperated, and I had to peel a few of them from the floor.

Armed with an old-fashioned stopwatch, I forced myself to keep all of my lessons under fifteen minutes. The results were encouraging: my students transitioned quickly and worked more efficiently at their tables when I kept these lessons short. But I soon detected another obvious problem: my students were sitting down nearly 100 percent of every class. Intuitively I knew this was problematic, and later I would find out why.

When I stopped to think of it, whenever I'd visit other schools in the States, I would see the same phenomenon. American students were being asked to sit for the majority of lessons. Not only that, but they weren't very active during the entire school day. And this could only mean that millions of children were missing out on the rich benefits of being more physically active. Research has shown that physical activity can fend off obesity, reduce the risk of cardiovascular disease, improve cognitive functions (such as memory and attention), and positively impact mental health (Walker, 2015).

I somewhat assumed that the lack of physical activity in schools was an American problem—a natural by-product of long school days and limited opportunities for recess. But when I started teaching in Finland, I saw the same thing happening at my public school in Helsinki. At first, this didn't add up. Kids in Finland have short school days and frequent fifteen-minute breaks. And even though the breaks keep them more focused in the classroom, they don't necessarily keep them more active at school.

On the playground, sunshine or snowfall, I'd find many

young Finnish children spending recess passively. Some would be tapping away on their smartphones, hooked by the latest mobile game, while others would be huddled together, sitting down on benches, or standing in small groups and chitchatting. Usually, I could find a handful of students playing tag or soccer. But the number of passive kids typically seemed to exceed the number of active ones. In the hallways of my school, older students were often slouched against the wall or even lying down, waiting for their next lesson to begin.

Finnish researchers confirmed my observations. On the "Finnish Report Card 2014 on Physical Activity for Children and Youth," kids in Finland received a D for overall physical activity levels. In 2013, one study revealed that only half of the participating Finnish elementary students met the national guideline of engaging in at least one hour of "moderate-to-vigorous" physical activities each day. Among middle school students, the figure was even worse: 17 percent (Walker, 2015).

Finland wasn't the only country that did poorly on its physical activity report card. On the "2014 United States Report Card on Physical Activity for Children and Youth," America received a D– for overall physical activity levels. Roughly a quarter of American children ages six through fifteen are active an hour per day on at least five days of the week, according to the report card (Walker, 2015).

Though children in both countries suffer from low activity levels, a key difference exists between Finland and the United States: hundreds of schools across this tiny Nordic nation are now endeavoring to keep kids active throughout the day through a relatively new government initiative called Finnish Schools on the Move. This experiment could serve as an example of what America could do to get kids more active.

Between 2010 and 2012, forty-five Finnish schools piloted the program. And the results were hopeful, demonstrating schools can increase the physical activity of children as long as they make the effort. According to a survey conducted after the pilot program, half of participating elementary school students and a third of middle school students reported an increase in physical activity (Walker, 2015).

Earth-shattering outcomes? No. "It takes some time for the actions taken to manifest and as a result, long-term and systematic development work is required to increase children's physical activity during the school day," said one summary of the pilot program. But humble as it was, Finnish Schools on the Move was a step in the right direction (Walker, 2015).

Tuija Tammelin, the research director of LIKES, the foundation that conducted the study of the pilot program, told me that she was impressed with the rapid adoption of Finnish Schools on the Move. In just a couple of years, the number of participating comprehensive schools had grown from forty-five to nearly eight hundred. In the fall of 2014 my school launched this initiative, and I was able to see Finnish Schools on the Move in action.

• • •

IT WAS JUST PAST NOON ON A MID-DECEMBER SCHOOL day, and I wandered outside during one of those fifteen-minute breaks. (This took place during my second year of teaching in Helsinki, when I looped with my Helsinki students to teach them in sixth grade.) Because my school had recently launched Finnish Schools on the Move, I wondered if anything had changed about my students' behavior. Would I see fewer kids slothing around the playground?

In neon-yellow vests, two of my sixth graders, Emmi and Marianne, were facilitating a popular game known as Banana Tag. Around them, about a dozen younger children were dashing back and forth.

Emmi and Marianne were "recess activators," meaning they were trained to work with their younger peers, especially first and second graders, once a week. A few minutes before I arrived, the two girls had huddled up with these seven- and eight-year-olds and decided on a game to play.

I walked up to Emmi during the middle of her game, and as the youngsters cheerfully zigzagged to avoid us, I asked her whether the little kids were more active during recess since she started leading these games. She gave me one of those looks kids give when adults ask them a question that has an obvious answer. With her eyebrows raised, she nodded vigorously—a cue that I should jump out of their way.

Eventually it became clear that what I had observed that day with Emmi and Marianne was a daily routine. Every day at noon, several recess activators engaged in similar activities, dispersing across the blacktopped playground and recruiting younger children to join them in active games like Banana Tag.

I visited another school in the Finnish city of Salo, a 1.5-hour drive from Helsinki. There, I found sixth graders helping out in a different way. A lesson had just ended, and I watched as dozens of elementary school students flocked to the foyer where their winter coats and outdoor shoes were kept. But instead of zooming outside, which might have been the case in the past, several children stayed behind and formed a straight line in front of a table near the front door. Each child grasped a slip of paper the size of a business card. These papers, I discovered, were "passports" granting them the right to borrow exercise equipment during recess.

A few moments later, two older students slid behind the table. With a key from the teacher's lounge, they unlocked the compartment underneath the table and called up the first child—a petite, blond-haired boy.

"What do you want?" one of the older kids chirped after collecting the boy's "passport." The boy asked for a basketball and, once it was presented, snatched it happily and rushed outside. Next, a round-faced brunette stepped up and requested a jump rope. And so it went until the long line of eager children disappeared.

Curious as to whether this program had been as successful as the one at my Helsinki school, I stepped up to the counter and asked the older students if they had also witnessed a change in the level of physical activity during break times. Their answer, unsurprisingly, was also yes.

But that wasn't enough to convince me that the program is producing results across the board. Although I saw younger children moving a lot during their breaks, I still wondered about the impact of Finnish Schools on the Move on older students. After all, the pilot program revealed that sedentary behavior at school increased steadily by age. Later surveys, moreover, reported that just a third of students in grades seven through nine increased their level of physical activity each day despite participating in the pilot (Walker, 2015).

So I caught up with one of the PE teachers at my Helsinki

school who was coordinating the program. Although she was pleased with the work of recess activators like Emmi and Marianne, she acknowledged that something needed to be done about the older children. But she had a plan.

My Helsinki school would transition to a different daily schedule that would be designed to allow students extra time to engage in the physical activities that interest them most. Instead of only providing short, fifteen-minute recesses, the school would offer at least one thirty-minute break on a daily basis. This change would especially benefit the students in grades seven through nine at my school, who have outgrown games like tag and need something more developmentally appropriate to get their heart rates up.

Under this new model, the older students would have the chance to come up with their own diversions to keep themselves active during the school day: yogalates, floor hockey, or gymnastics, to name a few of the possibilities. The kids get to dream it up; as long as it's something vigorous, it's an option. Students run and direct these activities—and that's intentional. Finnish schools are encouraging children to take ownership by inviting their ideas and carving out the time and space for these activities to happen at school.

But this model doesn't just underscore the value of student empowerment. It also demonstrates that increasing physical activity shouldn't be a goal reserved only for recess or PE class.

In fact, I've come to realize that class time should also involve physical activity. When my school's faculty introduced Finnish Schools on the Move, the coordinators came up with various strategies for getting students to be more active during lessons, for example, offering "energizers" (short breaks from sitting for students during lessons), allowing kids to complete work while standing, and replacing conventional chairs with exercise balls so that students can bounce and learn simultaneously.

Since that fall, I started searching for even more ways to activate my students during lessons. One of the strategies I experimented with is an adaptation of something I first observed in the United States: I call it the active gallery walk, which keeps kids moving yet ensures they're focused during class.

This tactic grew out of my frustration with a very traditional way of doing school. All too often, students present their work passively; they stand at the front of their classrooms with a poster or a slideshow presentation and lecture the class on what they've learned, for example. Not only does this common practice consume a lot of instructional time, but it's also (relatively) unproductive. Sitting down and listening to numerous presentations in a row can become eye-glazingly boring for everyone in the class—including the teacher—no matter how skillfully the students share their work.

While giving students the opportunity to present their learning is, of course, important, I'd argue that it's not worth doing if it's not engaging and active for kids, hence the active gallery walk. Here's how it works: Students fasten their presentations to the walls of the classroom or hallway as if they were exhibiting their work in an art gallery. Each display is numbered, and the children rotate from exhibit to exhibit systematically, spending a minute or two carefully studying each one. To make this experience more meaningful, students provide written feedback to one another as they're visiting each

display. Before they start the active gallery walk, I hand out
sticky notes in two different colors: on one color my students
write questions about the work for the presenter to consider,
and on the other they jot down positive observations.

And although they appear to bob happily throughout an
active gallery walk, as they lean in to view each presentation
and scrawl feedback on sticky notes, perhaps the best part
for them comes after the activity is over. They rush to take
down their presentations and return to their desks, where
they then scrutinize the feedback from their classmates. Naturally, I give them time to revise their work. And to my
delight, students have always chosen to improve their presentations without any prodding from me.

· · ·

HALFWAY THROUGH ONE OF THOSE ACTIVE GALLERY
walks with my Helsinki sixth graders, I checked my watch
and was amazed at how quickly time was flying by. Twenty
minutes had already passed, but it felt as if we had just
begun. Emmi turned around when she heard me exclaim
"wow!" and asked for an explanation. I showed her the
time, and like me, she couldn't believe the number of minutes that had elapsed. We agreed that learning should feel
this way all the time.

Jukka, another of my students, approached me after the
active gallery walk, gave me a high five, and thanked me for
the lesson. But in my mind his expression of gratitude—as if
I had just given Jukka and his classmates an unexpected
gift—seemed unwarranted. All students deserve active,
engaging lessons like the one he and Emmi just experienced.

Finnish Schools on the Move has helped me to see that schools in America—and around the world—can increase the physical activity of children by nudging all students to take ownership of their active lifestyles and encouraging us teachers to come up with creative ways of getting kids to move inside their classrooms.

Something like an active gallery walk can work at any grade level. Here are some other ideas for doing what the Finnish initiative aims to accomplish—increasing physical activity and reducing the amount of time that students are sitting. The following suggestions are partly derived from the Finnish Schools on the Move website (Liikkuva Koulu, n.d.):

- Look for ways to incorporate standing, or movement, somewhat naturally into lessons. If you're an elementary school teacher and you're reading a book to your students, ask the children to stand up and act out a small portion of the text as you're reading. In my second year of teaching in Helsinki, I worked with a second grade classroom and during a read-aloud of *Charlie and the Chocolate Factory,* we danced around the classroom while I read a long "Oompa Loompa" chant, for example. (The kids loved it, and it gave everyone a chance to stand up and move.) For older students, how about hosting "standing-room only" discussions? For added measure, you and the students could push the chairs and desks away from the middle of the classroom as you dive into the topic of the day.
- Sometimes, you might notice your students looking drowsy after sitting down for an extended period of time, despite your best efforts to keep lessons engag-

ing. During these occasions, why not get into charac-
ter (with your best army commander impression) and
call for an impromptu exercise break? Twenty jump-
ing jacks or twenty seconds of running in place could
breathe life into your lesson, while your students
receive that valuable break from sitting.

- If you're an elementary school teacher, you could
appoint "recess activators" in your classroom who
could carry out their duties on the playground on a
rotating basis, like my Helsinki students Emmi and
Marianne. I wouldn't force children to participate in
activator-led games, but as I've seen in Finland, providing students with daily opportunities to play fun,
active games like Banana Tag encourages them to be
much more physically active on the playground. If
you're considering this idea of appointing recess activators, I recommend you provide a little bit of training to those students by working with them to
compile a short list of games to lead and teaching
them how to support others as they play. Initially, it
would be important to supervise their beginning
attempts at facilitating, until they appear comfortable
in their roles.

- When I was teaching first and second graders in the
Boston area, I had one student—a small, restless
boy—who had trouble sitting properly. It seemed like
every time he was assigned to his table to complete
independent work, he wanted to stand. Eventually, I
eased up on directing him to sit, and in my opinion,
the quality of his work didn't suffer. While it's important for students, especially the young ones, to learn

proper handwriting technique and good posture, I think it's also valuable to give our students the freedom to move around, wiggle, and stand up. Some teachers, I've heard, have brought "standing desks" into their classrooms, and this seems like one good solution. But other, less expensive steps could be to allow students to read books while being on their feet, or provide clipboards for children to complete tasks while standing around the classroom.

Recharge after school

The regular full-time teaching load at my Helsinki school was only twenty-four hours each week, which translates—if fifteen-minute breaks are considered—as only eighteen hours of classroom instruction per week. This is a typical full-time teaching load for elementary school teachers in this Nordic country. At my previous school in America, my former colleagues and I would usually spend about 50 percent more time with students than teachers at my Helsinki school. In fact, U. S. teachers report the most hours (26.8), on average, of weekly classroom instruction compared to their OECD counterparts (Walker, 2016c).

Given that my Finnish colleagues were spending significantly fewer hours in the classroom, I expected, initially, that they'd spend significantly more hours of their free time working after school, prepping their classrooms, sending e-mails, and planning lessons. I thought this way because when I taught in the United States I used to dream of working a part-time schedule (something like a full-time teaching schedule in Finland), just so that I could spend more of my free time investing in my teaching.

But my Finnish colleagues surprised me. Typically, my school—a gigantic refurbished hospital building—appeared to be completely empty by 4:00 P.M.

During my first year in Helsinki, my wife was pregnant with our second child, and just one week before the baby's due date the principal confronted me one afternoon: "Shouldn't you be at home?"

Additionally, on a Friday at 3:30 P.M., I was working in an empty teachers' lounge, and the same principal whispered in my ear, "Time to go home."

Her words contrasted sharply with the message of an American principal I met in the Boston area. According to him, teachers could be categorized, basically, in two ways: those who worked late into the afternoon, and those who "beat the bus out of the parking lot." One group, he sug- gested, represented a group of committed professionals, while that other cohort fell far short.

Teaching in Finland has taught me that this dichotomy is inaccurate and unhelpful. Although I'd often see my col- leagues rushing home just minutes after their last classes would finish, I learned to view them as wise, not lazy, for lim- iting their hours of work. They knew the importance of leav- ing work to recharge, in order to stay strong as teachers.

Any teacher, with at least a full year of experience, knows that teaching is more like a marathon than a sprint. But based on what I've observed in American schools, it seems like many teachers, my old self included, have a difficult time pacing themselves, even when their bodies tell them to slow down.

During my rookie year in the Boston area I tried the sprinting approach, where I'd work until my head hit the pillow, cut my hours of sleep to arrive at school earlier, and prep during my lunch break. My nonstop working method led to a predictable outcome: I completely burned out, suffering from crippling anxiety, and I thought I'd leave the profession for good.

One of my biggest mistakes during that first year was the way I assessed myself. I figured that the *more* hours I worked, the *more* successful I would be as a teacher. And, for me, that just wasn't the case. I was working hard, but I wasn't working smart. In that first year, I'd often spend many hours after school fussing over classroom decorations or trying to script my lessons perfectly. What I needed, on most afternoons, was not another hour of prep but an extra hour or more of disconnecting from my work.

Once, I met with an American teacher visiting Helsinki who told me that at his public high school in Virginia he was required to clock in and clock out of school each day, as if he and his colleagues were working in the construction business. The strange thing, according to this teacher, was that the school district said the data would not impact evaluations in any way, and still teachers were required to use this time-keeping system. As he described this policy, I started to imagine the pressure that he and his colleagues would feel to clock in earlier and clock out later, even when it wasn't required. The emphasis in that school district, it seemed to me, was not on the quality of the teaching but on the *amount* of teaching.

To prioritize joy in our classrooms, we need to start pushing back on this unhelpful ideology, which tells us to assess ourselves based on how much we work. Indeed, American teachers work incredibly long hours compared to other teachers around the world, and this reality, in my opinion, should encourage U.S. teachers to allocate at least a portion of their limited free time on a daily basis to activities after school that refresh them.

I don't think it's self-serving to get recharged every day. What could be viewed as self-serving, ironically, is doing the opposite: working, working, working until we're stressed out, anxious, and unavailable to our students. The children look to us for stability, and when we're on a leave of absence (or on the path to burnout), we can't be there for them. In fact, forty-six percent of U.S. teachers say they encounter a large amount of daily stress, tied with America's nurses for the highest percentage among all professional categories (Walker, 2016b).

Recharging after school comes in different forms for different teachers. Some might be refreshed by a short run; others could find nourishment by playing trains with their toddlers; many probably enjoy just a few minutes of reading for leisure. The most important thing, I've found, is that boundaries—when to work and when to rest—are identified and kept. All teachers know their own workload, and all educators have "have-tos" in their schedules, so I'm not suggesting that we start shirking our responsibilities—I'm recommending that we put the emphasis on pacing ourselves.

Years ago, I spoke with one American teacher who told me that she'd aim to spend as much time as possible after school with her school-age children, and then, after they had fallen asleep, she'd plan lessons and return e-mails. For her, this routine worked well—she knew when she was recharging and when she was working. I prefer something a little different: I'd rather leave my work at school. That way, I can disconnect from teaching for the rest of the evening, even if it means returning home a couple hours later. In Helsinki, I aimed to leave school about two hours after my last lesson, because that deadline would usually provide me with just enough time to take care of the teaching essentials: planning the next day's lessons, preparing classroom materials, assessing student work, and clearing my e-mail inbox.

I've learned that I'm usually incapable of recharging after school if I've left essential schoolwork undone. My mind continues to ruminate on what needs to be accomplished, even if I'm engaged in a leisurely activity like playing with my children at home. Setting a deadline, I've found, nudges me to do the most important things first before leaving school. And once I have those basic items taken care of, I feel a healthy sense of confidence about the next day of teaching, which helps me to disconnect from work in the evening.

During the school year, it can be tempting to participate in exciting (but nonessential) initiatives like Twitter chats, volunteer committees, and book clubs. Those opportunities can be a lot of fun, of course, but they can also distract us from taking care of the essential teaching tasks, which would then reduce the already limited amount of free time we have for recharging. (Summer, I've found, is the best time for teachers to participate in these types of professional initiatives because we don't have to worry about preparing for that next day of school.)

But even when we set reasonable boundaries for ourselves, making sure to recharge on a daily basis, there are times when our jobs require incredibly long days. During the end-of-term report card season, which would happen twice each year at my Helsinki school, I'd often see my Finnish colleagues working late into the evening. The same thing would happen on special evenings, such as the annual Parent Night. There are some days when we don't have the chance to recharge after work, but when we're in the habit of recharging most days, we'll be ready for them.

. . .

ONCE WE GRASP THE VALUE OF REGULARLY RECHARGing our teaching batteries, I think we'll begin to see how important it is for our students, too. (It's especially valuable for kids in America, because long days of school already significantly diminish their available free time.)

As teachers, there's little that we can do to influence how the children in our classroom will spend their hours after school. That being said, there's one obvious area where we can encourage our students to recharge every day: homework.

It's been said many times before, on the Internet and elsewhere, that there's no homework in Finland. Sorry to disappoint you, but that's a popular myth. What I've found, though, is that Finnish teachers are reasonable about the amount of homework they assign their students. The ones I've spoken with don't want to overload kids with extra schoolwork, because they recognize the value of their free time. Surprisingly, Finnish teachers seem to hold this belief about keeping homework generally light, even when Finland's students have been recognized as having significantly fewer hours of classroom instruction than many of their peers in other developed nations.

In Finland, I've yet to encounter such a thing as a school homework policy. I've found that it's up to Finland's teachers to decide how much homework is appropriate for their students. In my experience, Finland's educators often assign (relatively) small homework tasks, which can be completed over the span of several days. Furthermore, the tasks are generally straightforward, allowing the students to complete them on their own without help from adults.

I think it's wise for us to think about keeping homework to a necessary minimum, so that our students can spend more time recharging in the evenings. If you work in a school in which you're required to assign a certain amount of homework each night, then one way you can help students to recharge in the evening is by keeping the homework tasks as simple as possible, so that students can complete them easily on their own.

Simplify the space

Once, as I was leading a tour of my Helsinki school for American visitors, one administrator turned to face me, with a slight look of concern. "I noticed there's not much on the walls," he said. That visitor wanted to know why.

The easy answer was that my Helsinki school was out for the summer, and many students, including my own, had taken their work home. But that wasn't the whole story. If you were to visit my school in May of that year, the sight wouldn't have been all that different. You would have found, I'd imagine, a set of posters students completed during a recent geography unit, or drawings that students created during their visual arts class. In my visits to other Finnish schools, I saw the same kinds of items being displayed. In my experience, teachers in Finland prefer to minimize the amount of stuff on the walls in their classrooms and the hallways. It's something that may come naturally to them.

The mantra "less is more" is often celebrated by the Finns, evidenced by the minimalism of Finnish design. Visit a Finnish home, and it's likely that you'll find an uncluttered, cozy space (think Ikea style). A nice compliment you can pay a Finnish host, I've found, is a positive remark about the home's *tunnelma* (atmosphere). In my years of living in Finland, I've learned that a cozy home, from a Finnish perspective, depends largely on keeping one's living space as simple as possible.

I think the same principle informs the design of Finland's classrooms. Many visitors who see Finnish schools in action notice the calmness of students and teachers. Surely there are many factors behind this phenomenon, but one reason for the lack of overwhelm, I believe, is the simplified learning space.

In 2014, researchers from Carnegie Mellon University explored this idea, investigating how a highly decorated classroom might sidetrack children from focusing on learning. In the study, kindergarten students were taught six introductory science lessons in a laboratory classroom, where researchers would experimentally change the learning environment—for some lessons, the walls were crowded with decorations, and at other times, the walls were completely bare. The study revealed that children "were more distracted by the visual environment, spent more time off task, and demonstrated smaller learning gains when the walls were highly decorated than when the decorations were removed" (Fisher, Godwin, & Seltman, 2014, p. 1362).

As teachers, reducing the external stimuli in our classrooms is especially important for young students, because the ability to focus is something that develops as children age. The authors of this study pointed out that sixth graders are able to ignore irrelevant stimuli much more easily than preschoolers (Hoffman, 2014).

Anna V. Fisher, the study's lead author, told *The New York Times* in an interview that academic results are affected by numerous factors, but many of them are beyond the control of educators. That being said, the appearance of a classroom is something that teachers can easily influence, the researcher noted (Hoffman, 2014).

Displaying high-quality student work can be a joyful endeavor. Students can (and should) feel proud of the good work they've done, and as educators we can be proud of the ways that we've shepherded them. At the same time, research suggests that there might be such a thing as overdoing it.

As teachers, I think we can sometimes become too focused on how learning *appears*. We can spend an inordinate amount of time obsessing about and affixing student work to our walls, when there are more essential aspects of teaching to attend to. With embarrassment, I remember I used to staple my first graders' math worksheets to the bulletin board, during my early years of teaching in the Boston area. A balance is needed, and yet I recognize that it may feel like a struggle to simplify your classroom.

Years ago, I met teachers from a public school in Massachusetts who told me that their school received scathing criticism for failing to display an adequate amount of student work, even though it was still early in the school year. The evaluators felt that the (mostly) bare walls suggested that there was a lack of student learning. So what do you think those teachers prioritized from that day forward?

This idea that paper on walls connotes good learning seems silly, in my opinion, because it's possible that a teacher could be spending a significant amount of classroom time directing students to complete wall decorations. That teacher's classroom may look impressive, but scratch beneath the surface and I suspect you will find a lack of meaningful learning taking place during the school day.

So how can teachers keep learning spaces simple, despite greater pressure, perhaps, to bombard classroom walls with evidence of learning? It starts with thinking through the purpose of displaying student work. Is it primarily for vanity's sake, the appearance of learning? If it is, I'm convinced, from my own experience in American classrooms, that it will ultimately burden us teachers, distracting us from our most essential work.

I'm not suggesting that teachers keep their classrooms completely bare. If we're purposeful about the stuff that goes up on the walls, there's joy there. But we probably need to exercise restraint because of external pressure. That urge to festoon the walls with paper might come from the perceived threat of tough evaluators, such as the ones I heard about in Massachusetts, but the pressure will most likely come from colleagues down the hall, who are affixing lots of paper to their walls, or parents, who seem to think that more stuff on display equates to better learning.

But we know, deep down, that showing off a lot of student work and posters doesn't necessarily mean that there's a lot of meaningful learning happening in our classrooms. One of the most important aspects of learning is thinking, and that is a messy, invisible process. In other words, not everything we do with our students can be packaged as evidence, ready for display.

One kindergarten teacher in California, Ingrid Boydston, confessed that she used to completely cover the walls of her classroom, but these days, according to *The New York Times*, she intentionally reserves empty spaces. When she taught a lesson on the French artist Claude Monet, she wore a smock and a wide-brimmed straw hat and talked to the children in the sort of European accent one would expect to hear on such an occasion. After completing her speech, she turned to a white-board and supplied it, *The New York Times* reported,

> with key words that her twenty-seven young students remembered from her talk. Then the children went to the room's paint center, where they went to work with cotton swabs.
>
> Finally, it was time to adorn a blank wall. Mrs. Boydston filled it with artwork: the children's Monets, not Claude's. (Hoffman, 2014)

As teachers, we have a responsibility to have an answer ready as to why we do counterintuitive things, such as keeping our classrooms simple. A colleague, a parent, or a student might ask, why are your walls so (relatively) bare? But instead of feeling attacked and embarrassed, we can calmly offer clear rationale. Here are my reasons:

- I want the walls of my classroom to exude a sacred quality to the children. When I say to my students, "I'm hoping that this work that you're doing will be displayed," I want that to mean something special. I want them to feel like it's an honor to get something displayed in our classroom. If I'm exhibiting a lack of discernment about what gets displayed, throwing (almost) everything on the walls, such as hastily completed homework assignments, the students get the opposite message. In my experience, they care less about what gets shown.

- Time is our most precious commodity as teachers, and because the supply is limited, I've chosen to restrict the amount of time I spend on something as auxiliary as classroom displays. That doesn't mean I don't value it. It simply means that I recognize that I have lots of competing responsibilities. One way to limit the time I invest in affixing work to the walls is to involve students. Even young children, in my experience, enjoy displaying their own work in the classroom. There's no reason, in my opinion, why a teacher should be spending his or her time after school displaying the work of students. Recruiting students to help in this way, during the school day, saves us valuable time and promotes greater ownership of their learning.
- Displaying less stuff will, undoubtedly, put a greater emphasis on the few items displayed on the wall. That's a very good thing.
- Putting up less stuff will reduce the external stimuli in the classroom, and it could, according to research, help the students to stay focused.

The decision to keep our classrooms uncluttered is something, in my experience, that can ultimately save us time, facilitate higher-quality work, and promote less distracted teaching and learning. And if you keep the learning environment simple, I predict that when you stand in the middle of your classroom and spin around, surveying its walls, you won't feel overwhelmed or shameful about the relative lack of stuff on display. You'll feel, along with your students, a sense of joy.

Breathe fresh air

When I visited Minna Räihä and her sixth grade classroom in Kuopio, Finland, I noticed something I probably would have missed if I didn't have those two years of teaching in Helsinki. As we chatted during a break, this veteran teacher interrupted me, midsentence: "I need to open a window." She rushed over to one of the classroom windows to let in more fresh air. I chuckled, because it was a familiar sight.

My Helsinki students were often opening the windows in our classroom, without asking permission. Sometimes, I'd hear something like "I need some fresh air" and I'd know that one of my students was making a move to the windows. In hindsight, I see why several of my pupils were often concerned with the air quality. Our classroom, formerly a dentist's office, was tiny and barely fit the twenty-five of us. The learning space was stuffy unless the windows were open.

My Helsinki students seemed much more aware of air quality than I had ever been. In my several years of teaching in the United States, I had never thought to open the windows in the classrooms where I taught to let in fresh air. It was such a little, simple thing, but my students (and other teachers in Finland, like Minna) were helping me to see its importance.

Although research suggests that brain breaks are useful indoors or outdoors (Walker, 2014), the Finnish students and teachers that I've chatted with typically commend the value of going outside to get fresh air. This philosophy is perhaps most visible in the policies of many Finnish schools, where elementary school students are required to head outdoors unless it's colder than −15°C (5°F). That means a rainy day isn't an excuse for staying indoors for a break. During my first year of teaching in Helsinki, I remember looking out the window on one autumn day and feeling a bit shocked as I watched scores of children running around the playground in the rain. As my Finnish father-in-law often likes to say, "We're not sugar."

At Kalevala Comprehensive School, where Minna works, teachers and students partly condition the air the "natural" way by opening classroom windows. "In Finland, there [are] very clear regulations about how many pupils you can take in a certain space," Minna told me. "It's been calculated by the officials that if you have so and so many square meters [and] so much height in the classroom, then you can only take so and so many pupils."

But Finland's appreciation for fresh air wasn't just a school thing. For example, I saw Helsinki parents leaving their sleeping infants in strollers on their balconies, even in freezing temperatures. When I asked Finns about this, they'd often remark that babies nap better outside. (We did the same with our youngest child in Helsinki, and it was something I'd never imagine doing in America.)

In Finland, all the talk about fresh air got me questioning if I had been missing out for years on a simple strategy for better well-being and better learning in the classroom. During my visit to the Kalevala Comprehensive School, I asked

Minna about the benefits of fresh air, and she provided me with a brief science lesson as we chatted by her desk: "When we inhale, we [exhale] carbon dioxide. And if the level of carbon dioxide becomes too high in the classroom, it really stops learning—because your [brain doesn't] work!"

Minna's finding seems to agree, partly, with a research finding involving office workers. In this study, two dozen professionals worked for fourteen days in two rooms, where air quality could be manipulated remotely to resemble the environment of a standard office building, a "green building," or a green building with enhanced ventilation ("green+"). Every afternoon those participants took cognitive tests on computers. The results showed that cognitive function scores were significantly higher when the participants worked in the two environments with better than conventional air quality; the results, on average, were 61 percent better during a green building session and 101 percent better during a green+ session (Higgins, 2015). Although the experiment was created to simulate indoor office spaces, the researchers concluded: "These exposures should be investigated in other indoor environments, such as homes, schools, and airplanes, where decrements in cognitive function and decision making could have significant impacts on productivity, learning, and safety" (Allen et al., 2016, p. 812).

When I told Minna about the study of the office workers, she didn't seem surprised at all. "There are so many things in the environment that . . . affect the learning," she said. In my own research for this book, I've found several other environmental factors that influence learning, several of which I discuss in these chapters: classroom decorations, noise, insufficient lighting, and poor heating. "[A] plethora of scientific

evidence suggests that student learning and achievement
[are] deeply affected by the environment in which this learning occurs," wrote the authors of a research review (Cheryan,
Ziegler, Plaut, & Meltzoff, 2014, p. 10), which investigated
how the physical classroom environment influences student
performance. While teachers have little control over the
structural design of the schools where they teach, there are
small things we can do to make the physical classroom environment better for our students. Here's a useful list, based on
several recommendations provided by the researchers in a
2014 press release by Sage Publications:

- When students are exposed to more natural light,
  they perform better. With this finding in mind, seek
  to minimize artificial lighting in your classroom.
- According to the researchers, the temperature range
  of 68°F and 74°F is optimal for learning. So, while
  opening the classroom windows during the winter
  might benefit air quality, the cold temperature might
  hinder student achievement.
- Researchers have discovered that classroom objects
  showing educational accomplishments of traditionally
  disadvantaged groups (such as posters that depict
  female scientists) can bolster the performance of such
  groups.
- Displaying "token" symbols in the classroom setting,
  such as American Indian mascots, can lead students of
  such groups to report lower self-esteem.

Informed by the findings of these researchers, the Department of Computer Science and Engineering at the Univer-

sity of Washington redesigned its facilities (including the computer lab), and its faculty and students have responded positively, suggesting that the learning environment has become more inclusive and success oriented (Sage Publications, 2014). As teachers at the K-12 level, we can do something similar by tweaking our classroom environments.

Get into the wild

Last spring, as I was walking my dog around the pond behind our home in Finland, I discovered several boys, in fourth grade or so, fishing on their own. As the days got sunnier, I continued to notice more and more Finnish children outside without adults—riding their bikes, swimming in nearby ponds, and walking around with fishing poles. But it wasn't just the warm weather that brought kids out to explore nature. I saw something similar during the coldest season.

In the winter I'm in the habit of running around a larger pond by our home, which is typically frozen, and one morning I was surprised to find about fifty children on the ice, cross-country skiing with their teachers. Those students looked like they were in first or second grade. On another occasion, on that same frozen pond, I saw teenage students ice fishing with their teacher. On a separate day, on a hill next to the pond, I found elementary school students sledding during the school day. (Their teachers approved—they were the ones supervising.) Just a few hundred yards from that hill I visited a kindergarten, where teachers told me that they'd sometimes visit a nearby forest where their students would learn math concepts.

One of the most beloved part of elementary school in

Finland—for many children, at least—is something called "Camp School," in which Finland's fifth graders or sixth graders, typically, spend several days with their teachers in a natural setting. For Camp School, my students and I took an hour and a half bus ride away from Helsinki to spend a few days at an athletic retreat center, where we completed a variety of fun, physically demanding activities. Last year, Minna Räihä took her sixth grade students on several Camp School excursions.

In my experience, Finland's teachers seem eager to bring their kids outside of their classrooms. In his 2008 book *Last Child in the Woods*, Richard Louv praises this Nordic nation for encouraging environment-based education, in which Finland "has moved a substantial amount of classroom experience into natural settings or the surrounding community" (p. 205). Louv is best known for coining the term *nature-deficit disorder* to communicate the yawning gap between kids and nature (Louv, 2011). In light of nature-deficit disorder, Louv (2008) suggests that America adopt Finland's commitment to environment-based education.

Initially, I felt reluctant to include the strategy *get into the wild*, because I wondered if it was too Finland-centric. In this Nordic country, it's relatively easy to enjoy and explore nature. Pull up a satellite image of Finland, and you will see a nation that's almost completely covered with trees and lakes. I questioned whether educators around the world, especially those teaching in urban school districts, could realistically practice this strategy. But then I remembered that connecting regularly with the natural world is vital for everyone. Once, I visited a forest kindergarten in my Finnish city, where a group of five- and six-year-old children spent about four hours outside each day (on average) and, afterward, I emailed Louv to help me understand the benefits of such an arrangement.

"The research strongly suggests that time in nature can help many children learn to build confidence in themselves; reduce the symptoms of Attention Deficit Hyperactivity Disorder, calm children, and help them focus," Louv said in an email. "There are some indications that natural play spaces can reduce bullying. It can also be a buffer to child obesity and overweight, and offers other psychological and physical health benefits" (Walker, 2016a).

Improved cognitive functioning, Louv added, has been associated with nature-based learning for years. For a recent example, he pointed to a 6-year study involving more than 900 public elementary schools in Massachusetts, in which researchers found a link "between the greenness of the school in the spring (when most Massachusetts students take the [state-wide] tests) and school-wide performance on both English and Math tests, even after adjustment for socioeconomic factors and urban residency" (quoted in Walker, 2016a).

Time spent in nature, Louv told me, is "obviously not a cure-all" for children, however, he suggested that something like a forest kindergarten could "be an enormous help, especially for kids who are stressed by circumstances beyond their control" (Walker, 2016a).

As Louv points out in *Last Child in the Woods*, the idea of environment-based education is nothing new—it has been around for more than a hundred years. John Dewey, in his 1899 book *The School and Society*, supported this concept: "Experience [outside the school] has its geographical aspect, its artistic and its literary, its scientific and its historical sides. All studies arise from aspects of the one earth and the one life lived upon it" (quoted in Louv, 2008, p. 203). More recently, as Louv notes in his book, Howard Gardner—professor of education at Harvard University and the researcher who developed the theory of multiple intelligences—added another kind of intelligence to his list: "naturalist intelligence" (Louv, 2008).

For many teachers, especially ones in urban schools, taking students cross-country skiing or ice fishing isn't feasible. So where should educators begin? I find it helpful to think about several different tiers of getting students into the wild, from a (relatively) low level to a high level of investment. The first tier is about bringing nature *into* the classroom. The possibilities are near endless, depending on your curriculum. For example, while I taught elementary school students in America, we sprouted potatoes in different parts of the classroom for a unit on the scientific method, cared for tadpoles for a unit on the frog life cycle, and (under microscopes) studied pond water, which we retrieved from a nearby reservoir.

The second tier involves stepping *outside* for a lesson, or part of a lesson. Logistically, it's easiest when you don't need to arrange a field trip. Big excursions (for example, hiking a mountain or visiting an arboretum) are wonderful, but they often require a significant amount of management on behalf of the teacher. Using the schoolyard as a habitat is an effective way of getting students to interact with nature on a regular basis without investing a substantial amount of time planning. These are a few activities I used to do with my elementary school children in the Boston area: writing down observations and wonderings in science journals about natural objects (such as stones, pinecones, and feathers) found in the school yard, documenting wildlife around the school premises using digital cameras and uploading those photos to our online field guide, and collecting natural objects, such as decomposing leaves and large rocks, to use in our tadpole habitats. I recommend thinking about what useful natural sites might be within walking distance of your school. In the Boston area, I taught at one elementary school that was just a half-mile away from a pond, and there we gardened, documented wildlife (which we uploaded to our digital field guide), collected pond samples to study in our classroom, and raced different rubber ducks in a stream for a math and science lesson.

The third tier involves greening the school grounds by undertaking projects. "[Schools] might begin with butterfly gardens, bird feeders and baths, tree planting, or native plant gardens," writes Louv (2008, p. 219). "Moving on to larger projects, they can create ponds, nature trails, or restore streams." Years ago, I worked at an urban school in Massachusetts where a second grade teacher led her class to develop and maintain a large school garden. This undertaking was a major source of joy (and healthy pride) for that friend and her young students. At another school, I taught with a teacher who set up bird feeders outside of the classroom windows, where our students could easily observe and identify birds throughout the school year. The children's enthusiasm for these winged creatures was sky-high, and it appeared to motivate them as readers, writers, and learners.

As teachers, we don't need to make ambitious efforts to reap the benefits of environment-based education. We can take baby steps, experiencing the joy of making connections from our classrooms to the natural world.

Keep the peace

In eastern Finland I visited Haapaniemi Elementary School, and the principal, Jussi Kukkola, took me on a brief tour, showing me a couple of classrooms in action. I found a remarkable sense of calm there—both teachers and students seemed incredibly relaxed and unhurried, especially as they worked with their shoes off (a tradition in Finnish homes and schools). The principal told me that, starting in the fall of 2016, corresponding with the implementation of the latest national core curriculum, his school would be launching a new set of rules. Safety was the first one, he noted. But what was the purpose of the new rules? "To create a peaceful school environment," Kukkola told me.

This struck me. Here was a Finnish school that already seemed to excel in this area of offering a calm atmosphere for teachers and students, but this principal signaled that it should remain a priority. In America, I had heard of schools aiming to be rigorous, or project based, or high achieving. But peaceful? That was a new one for me.

In visits to other classrooms in Finland, I had noticed a similar peaceful atmosphere. I wasn't the only one who noticed this common characteristic. At my Helsinki school, we'd often have visitors from abroad, and I'd hear them comment on the same thing: the learning seemed so relaxed and so stress-free. I believe that this typical feature of peacefulness in Finnish schools is a major reason that Finland's students learn so efficiently and have performed so well on international tests like the PISA. "Learning is supported by a peaceful and friendly working atmosphere," declares Finland's newest curriculum framework (Finnish National Board of Education, 2016, p. 31), "and a calm, peaceful mood."

This respect for peace is something that's also evident in the Finnish language, in which several words describe occasions in which peace should be kept, *saunarauha* (sauna peace), *ruokarauha* (food peace), and *joulurauha* (Christmas peace), for example. This appreciation for tranquility is especially apparent during Finland's Independence Day celebration. Unlike the Fourth of July, in which crowds of people gather to watch booming fireworks, the Finnish holiday is observed by lighting candles in the quiet of one's home and remembering fallen soldiers.

In American classrooms, I've detected a healthy push for less teacher talk and more active learning; "turn-and-talk," for example, appears to be a popular strategy, in which students process their thinking out loud with one another. I wonder, though, if many American students are missing out on important moments of calm in the classroom because of this pedagogical trend of activating learning. While working silently may not qualify as active learning, I think there's wisdom in the approach of many Finnish classrooms I've observed, where children can have long stretches of time—while completing independent work—to work quietly.

Recently, I stumbled upon a body of research that seems to suggest the importance of this practice. Decades ago, University of Oregon researchers identified a relationship between the noisiness of a child's place of residence and a child's ability to detect the difference between two alike words and reading proficiency. In their experiment, they found that the louder the home environment, the more difficult it was for children to identify two similar words and read proficiently. More recently, University of Wisconsin researchers found something similar in a classroom setting: when there's background noise, very young children struggle to acquire novel words (Khazan, 2016).

In her article "How Noise Pollution Impairs Learning," Olga Khazan (2016), an *Atlantic* staff writer, described this compelling research, involving 106 toddlers:

> First, a group of 2-year-olds were taught two nonsense words . . . in the presence of background noise that was either 5 or 10 dB quieter than the voice of the teacher. The children successfully learned the words when the background noise was quiet, but not when it was loud.

Khazan noted that the result was identical in the second test, in which the researchers ran an experiment with toddlers who were a bit older. A third test revealed that the young children were able to acquire the definitions of novel words when exposed to loud background sounds, as long as they had first encountered them when the learning environment wasn't noisy.

Although further studies are needed to explore the impact of noise on learning (especially on older children), the research suggests that background noise in our classrooms can influence student learning. As a teacher, this encourages me to ensure that my classroom is a place of peace for students.

This section's strategy, *keep the peace,* is about promoting the well-being of everyone in the classroom through offering a calm learning environment, where students can work with little background noise and a lack of stress. The following are a few possible solutions for keeping the peace.

Anchor charts: A sensible starting place is the creation of rules, made by the teacher and the students. I've worked with each of my groups of students (in America and Finland) to craft a list of classroom rules, guided by the Responsive Classroom approach. The process is simple: typically during that first or second week of school, I solicit their ideas for shared classroom expectations and then guide them to whittle down a (usually) long list of rules to just a few overarching precepts. Typically, our rules boil down to three things: respect yourself, respect others, and respect the environment. While it's useful to have only three rules (it's easy to remember), I've often found that my students, even upper elementary ones, benefit from creating "anchor charts" together, which further flesh out the rules. The purpose of an anchor chart is to make classroom expectations clear as day by describing specific actions each student can take toward a particular goal, such as listening well, or, for the sake of this strategy, preserving a peaceful learning environment.

To make an anchor chart with your students, you need about ten to fifteen minutes for a discussion, a sheet of paper (or poster board), and something to write with. The layout is straightforward: the intended goal is at the top of the paper, and several questions are printed, which guide the discussion. The teacher can solicit ideas from students and write them down throughout the session. The purpose of this exercise is to get students to identify the characteristics of a peaceful learning environment. Once an anchor chart is made, the teacher and students can refer to it throughout the year. Here's an example:

The Peaceful Classroom

What does it look like?   Student A: "It's not messy. It's organized."

What does it sound like?   Student B: "It's quiet."

What does it feel like?   Student C: "Cozy."

Noise meter: Creating common expectations around this idea of a peaceful learning environment (though rules and an anchor chart) is important, but it's likely that our students will need ongoing feedback to know how they're doing, especially regarding minimizing background noise. One idea is that the class could have its own student-made "noise meter" prominently displayed at the front of the classroom, which teachers and students could regularly use to indicate the noise level of the classroom. I'm imagining that it would be best to get students to take ownership of this aspect, because from my own experience it's tempting for the teacher to assume the role of regulating the sound. And when this happens, students don't learn to self-regulate because they begin to depend on the teacher to intervene when they're too noisy.

Strike a balance: While I appreciate the quietness I've observed in many Finnish classrooms, where I've seen a lot of independent work, there's also a definite need for all students to discuss ideas and collaborate on a regular basis, too. One way of striking a balance is to offer opportunities for both. For example, students can work quietly at their desks while those students who need to discuss an idea, get feedback, or collaborate on something else can visit a designated spot in the classroom, where they won't disturb the peace.

· · ·

TODAY, ONE OF THE HOTTEST TRENDS IN CLASSROOMS around the world is practicing something called "mindfulness." When I first heard about this practice, I admit that I was skeptical. (Honestly, I thought it sounded pretty hokey.) But as I've read more and more about the benefits of this approach (and the relatively small investment of classroom time), it seems like a practice worth implementing in any classroom. Not only do mindfulness exercises help kids to remain attentive, according to researcher Amanda Moreno, but also students recover more quickly if they become unsettled and have an easier time transitioning throughout the school day (Deruy, 2016). One study, in an elementary school setting, found that children who received a mindfulness-based program not only bettered their "stress physiology" and "cognitive control," but they also:

(b) reported greater empathy, perspective-taking, emotional control, optimism, school self-concept, and mindfulness, (c) showed greater decreases in self-reported symptoms of depression and peer-rated aggression, (d) were rated by peers as more prosocial, and (e) increased in peer acceptance (or sociometric popularity). (Schonert-Reichl et al., 2015, p. 52)

During the 1970s, the biologist Jon Kabat-Zinn introduced the term mindfulness and he "defines it," wrote Lauren Cassani Davis (2015) for *The Atlantic*, "as a state of mind: the act of 'paying attention on purpose' to the present moment, with a 'non-judgmental' attitude. But mindfulness is really a secular philosophy and set of techniques adapted from thousands-of-years-old Buddhist meditation traditions . . ."

In the classroom setting, mindfulness exercises can vary, but they typically last just a few minutes, or even seconds. In New York City, one high school teacher, Argos Gonzalez, schedules five-minute mindfulness breaks in his English lessons, where students might conjure up mental images of their emotions or pay attention to inhaling and exhaling (Davis, 2015). In Patricia Jennings's 2015 book *Mindfulness for Teachers*, she suggests several simple exercises (appropriate for all students) that are "intended to promote self-awareness; foster cognitive, emotional, and behavioral self-regulation; and reduce stress" (p. 176).

• • •

ACCORDING TO JENNINGS, ONE OF THE MOST COMMON mindfulness-based practices is "mindful listening," and the only thing that's needed is a bell or a chime. This exercise seems especially useful when implemented during transitions, such as returning to the classroom after lunch or just before dismissal. Jennings recommends that teachers employ these words as they teach the routine of mindful listening:

> "We're going to do a listening activity that will help our minds relax and become more focused. First, let's all sit up nice and tall in our seats with our hands folded in our laps (or on the desk). In a few minutes, I'm going to ring this chime, and we're going to listen to the sound until it disappears. I find that I can focus my attention on my hearing best when I close my eyes. You can try that, but if you aren't comfortable closing your eyes, you can lower your gaze to your hands." (p. 177)

Once all of the students appear ready, the teacher can ring the bell, and when the ringing stops, the teacher can begin the lesson (Jennings, 2015).

Another effective mindfulness-based activity Jennings recommends to help students transition is called "mindful walking." When introducing this exercise, it's best if students have plenty of space to move around, such as the gym or the playground. Jennings advises teachers to introduce this activity in the following way:

> "Today we're going to practice paying attention to how we walk. I will show you how." Demonstrate walking slowly and describe how your weight shifts from the heel to the ball and then to the toe of your foot. "Pay attention to the feeling of the weight of your body on the soles of your feet." Have the students all face the same way and begin slowly walking in a cir-

cle. After a few minutes, stop and ask them how that feels. They may notice that it's not so easy to walk slowly. (p. 178)

Once these mindfulness-based routines have been mastered, Jennings recommends "[weaving] them into the fabric of your day," which will "create regular spaces in the day for everyone to calm down" (p. 176).

Belonging

ONE OF THE PRIMARY INGREDIENTS OF HAPPINESS, according to the academic literature, is belonging (Pinsker, 2016). And as teachers, there are different steps we can take to cultivate that sense of connectedness in our classrooms.

Recruit a welfare team

Belonging, by the way, is not just something that we can share with our students—it's also something that, as teachers, we need to experience with other adults, in school and out of school. Before diving into the six other strategies of this chapter, which focus on strengthening relationships between teachers and students, I want to affirm the importance of cultivating a supportive community of adults, something I learned personally during my burnout year.

In my round-the-clock striving to teach well, I found that my connections with others greatly suffered, including the ones with my colleagues, my friends, and even my family. Simply put, I wasn't prioritizing relationships. I was barely investing in them, and consequentially, I felt isolated in my work.

It wasn't until after I returned from that embarrassing leave of absence that I understood how much I had missed from being disconnected from others. And when I started to invest more time in relationships, I found the sense of belonging returning.

At my Helsinki school, I witnessed my colleagues prioritizing connections with one another in a way I hadn't observed in many American schools. One major reason for this phenomenon is probably a difference in the teaching schedule. (With shorter days and more breaks throughout the day, Finland's teachers have more free time to meet with one another.) But I also think it has to do with a particular attitude, which I discuss more in Chapter 5, that views the job of teaching as a collaborative endeavor.

I've heard some American educators describe teaching as a lonely job, in the sense that teachers spend a lot of time with their students but little time with other adults. I don't think this description would accurately describe the reality in many Finnish schools. In my experience, Finland's teachers spend a lot of time with one another at school, sharing best practices, problem solving, and developing friendships.

If we are committed to recharging after school (on a

daily basis) *and* if we recognize that belonging has a positive effect on our happiness and our teaching, then it would
be sensible to regularly use a portion of our free time
investing in connections with other adults. For me, that
would look like eating lunch with my colleagues regularly
(not skipping the meal to prep in my classroom), catching
up with a good friend over the phone in the late afternoon,
or drinking tea with my wife after our children have fallen
asleep.

In addition to investing time in relationships with other
adults, I recommend that we teachers practice an adaptation
of something that's implemented throughout this Nordic
country, including my Helsinki school: meeting with a "student welfare team." In Finland, a classroom teacher gathers
with other school professionals—the principal, the nurse, the
social worker, the psychologist, and the special education
teacher—as needed to discuss the individual needs of their
classrooms. Before my first meeting with my school's welfare
team, a Finnish colleague praised this powerful practice by
suggesting that I'd walk away from this gathering feeling
that I'm not the only one responsible for my students.

Before this meeting, I completed a brief survey, which
asked me several questions about the academic and social
needs of my students, and during our meeting I distributed
copies of my responses. As my colleagues quietly glanced
over the filled-in questionnaire, my principal turned to me
and asked, "So, how's your class so far?"

She had inquired about my class before, but this time, this
simple question seemed to possess special significance. It
was still early in the school year (October), and in that room
I found myself surrounded by a diverse crowd of school pro-

fessionals, ready to listen and respond to my insights. My principal was asking me to share the responsibility of caring for my class, so that the needs of my students would be better addressed. By the end of the meeting, we agreed upon several clear action items. I left the meeting feeling the way that my colleague predicted I would: less alone as a teacher.

Later that day, I checked my school e-mail and I found a message from another teacher, informing me about a concerning incident that took place among several of my students. I was upset by the news, but I had a plan. The next morning at school, I knocked on the door of the social worker's office, and I sought advice on this issue. She had a few moments to spare, and we had our first one-on-one meeting. The idea of sharing greater responsibility with my colleagues was crystallizing in me.

In Helsinki, I think I was starting to view my classroom in a helpful way. It wasn't just *my* classroom; it was *our* classroom. For many American teachers, I think that feeling of loneliness is a sign that we need to be better connected with other school professionals. And, while Finnish schools have student welfare teams that meet on a regular basis to support this need, I think any teacher can adopt a similar practice.

I'm imagining that teachers could call upon—without too much inconvenience—a small, trusted group of professionals and request a short meeting with them, once or twice a year, to discuss the academic and social-emotional needs of their classrooms. It would be like an annual checkup at the doctor's office. Getting that outside perspective on your classroom, I've learned, is so valuable, especially in the beginning of the school year.

Some teachers may be interested in recruiting team members beyond their own schools, and I think this could work well. Because teachers would be discussing their students during a welfare meeting, maintaining privacy is essential—and it's something that still can be honored, in my opinion, as long as the children are discussed anonymously.

If you're interested in promoting joy in your teaching, cultivating your personal sense of belonging is essential. And my hunch is that those teachers who maintain strong connections with other adults may find it easier to implement the following six strategies for strengthening a strong sense of belonging in the classroom: *know each child, play with your students, celebrate their learning, pursue a class dream, banish the bullying, and buddy up.*

Know each child

Before they became my fifth graders, my group of Helsinki students had been with the same classroom teacher for four years—first grade through fourth grade. And I could see, during those early days of the new school year, that their rapport with their previous teacher was exceptionally strong. On the first day of school, in the cafeteria, I watched many of my fifth graders laugh with and hug their former teacher. (Throughout Finnish elementary schools, the practice of a teacher remaining with a group of children for more than one school year is common.)

In Helsinki, I further understood the wisdom of this Finnish practice when I remained with my group of students for two years, starting in fifth grade. When I returned to teach them in sixth grade, I was impressed with how quickly we could reestablish healthy expectations and routines in our classroom. Not only that, but I found that, with another year with my class, my knowledge of them as unique individuals brought joy to our classroom and greatly benefited my teaching and their learning.

As teachers, we know it takes time to get to know our students well, but for many educators around the world, it seems as if they're forced to wave a permanent goodbye to the children at the end of each school year, just when they've finally established strong rapport with them. While it's relatively rare—in my experience—to find educators in America who "loop" with their students, just like teachers in Finland, there are simple steps to speed up the process of building strong teacher-student relationships.

One practice, which I implemented for the first time in Finland, is as straightforward as standing by the door and greeting students by name as they enter the classroom. I prefer to exchange fist bumps, handshakes, or high fives, too. Some of my Helsinki students would sometimes, playfully, try to sneak past me without a greeting—and it became our fun inside joke. This routine is something that allows teachers to recognize each student, signaling that we see them as individuals, not simply as a group of kids. During those brief moments by the door, I'd sometimes compliment a student on a new haircut or inquire about a sporting event. They were little things, just to say "I see you." If I was ending the day with my students, I would try to conclude the day in the same way I began it. Often I'd stand by our classroom door, ready to send them off with a cheerful farewell.

Many American elementary school teachers set aside time for a regular morning circle, where members of the classroom greet one another in different ways, such as shaking a neighbor's hand or chanting a choral greeting. Although I'm a strong proponent of morning circle, which is something I've used in my teaching since I started my career, I think we need to focus, too, on cultivating personal connections, on a daily basis, with each of our students. Morning circle, I've found, is especially effective at promoting a sense of joyful community in the classroom, rather than strengthening the individual relationships between teachers and students.

Another simple practice I utilized in Finland, which helped me to connect personally with my students, was eating lunch with them. At my Helsinki school, teachers were required to supervise their classes during lunch, so it wasn't difficult for me to share a meal with my class. It did require a little intentionality, though. Typically, teachers—during my lunch block—could elect to sit at a table with one another or at a table with a few of their students. I tried to alternate between those two options, because I found that it was important to invest time in relationships with both my colleagues and the children in my class. Although our lunch break was only twenty minutes long, it provided me with enough time to have casual conversations with my students. Often we'd exchange jokes and discuss our hobbies and interests. Occasionally, I'd get questions about life in America.

Because all twenty-five of us wouldn't fit around one table, I'd try to visit with different students throughout any given week. Typically, individual students would invite me to join them for lunch—and if I couldn't join them that day, I'd agree to eat with them on a separate occasion. Having those nonacademic moments at lunch, where we could freely discuss anything, was so valuable for strengthening our personal relationships.

In the classroom, I've found that, as teachers, it's important to model focused intensity during lessons, so that our students know it's time to focus intently on the learning, but I've seen that those occasions of just slowing down with students—at lunch, for example—are essential, too.

In Finland, it might be easier to arrange eating lunch with your students, given a difference in school policy, but I've met a few teachers in America implementing this practice, too. What's great about this simple gesture is that it will not only facilitate better rapport but also give you time to model respectful conversations and good eating habits, things that will also benefit your students. Eating with your students every day could be exhausting, even if you could, hypothetically, make it work. In my experience, I've found that there are days when I crave a few minutes to catch up with my colleagues or eat quietly in the corner, where I have a few minutes to reflect on a challenging morning. Striking a balance is essential.

If you're interested in the idea of eating with your students, I recommend starting small. Initially, you could try setting aside *one* lunch block each week to sit with several students. Because it's important to eat with each of your students eventually, it might be helpful to have a simple system for keeping track of who you're sitting with and when.

In addition to greeting our students and eating lunch with them, there's something we can do outside of school that can have a profoundly positive impact on our relationships with the children in our classroom: home visits. In

Helsinki I didn't think to conduct home visits because I wasn't available to meet with my fifth graders before the school year began in mid-August, but I believe it's a practice that would work well anywhere in the world.

While I taught in America, I conducted several home visits during the summer, and I found that, although it required a sacrifice of my time, it was well worth the investment. The most challenging part, I learned, was arranging the visits in advance, because families can be hard to reach during vacation season. But once I had a home visit planned, the actual event required very little preparation. The only thing I'd bring along was a pen and a notebook. Inside of my notebook, I had a list of questions to consider during the visit, which was something that my American mentor teacher gave me. Questions could range from "What are the child's hobbies?" to "What are the child's expectations for this school year?"

The actual visit consisted of two parts. First, I'd casually spend time with the student, chatting, and, if they wanted, I'd get a brief tour of their home to hear what they find most meaningful. Next, I'd meet with the guardians, when I could hear their insights on their child, along with finding out their wishes for the school year.

One of the greatest benefits of the home visit is the way it signals to students and their guardians that we care about getting to know each child. I think home visits are especially useful for teachers who have only a year with a particular group of children, because those educators—unlike many Finnish teachers—lack the possibility of getting to know students and their parents over the course of several years.

These simple practices—routinely greeting students,

regularly eating lunch with them, and conducting home visits—are just several ways of deepening teacher–student relationships. I believe that teachers who are committed to getting to know their students will inevitably develop an assortment of methods (like the ones I've mentioned) for getting to know their students better, which will ultimately contribute to the children's sense of belonging—and, consequentially, the overall level of joy in their classrooms.

Play with your students

Initially, I doubted whether I would ever survive at a Finnish school, given the high-performing kids and the well-trained teachers, but my confidence lifted when I recalled one area of preparation I had received in the United States: how to begin the school year. When I packed my luggage for our move to Helsinki in 2013, I made sure to bring my trusty college textbook, *The First Days of School.*

"Your success during the school year," wrote Harry Wong and Rosemary Wong (2009) in this classic American teaching guide, "will be determined by what you do on the first days of school" (p. 2). In my copy of the book, I had written an enthusiastic "true!" in the margins and circled this sentence in pencil. "You must have everything ready and organized when school begins," advised the authors (p. 6).

Like many American teachers I had known, I had taken this philosophy to heart—to such an extent that I had been in the habit of crafting detailed, minute-by-minute lesson plans for the first few days of school since my first year of teaching in Massachusetts. These plans were mostly centered on teaching my elementary school students important procedures and routines, such as those for fetching paper and visiting the restroom. So, in an effort to make "everything ready and organized" for that big, first day of school in Finland, I did what I had always done as a teacher in America: I spent summer days filling my planner and arranging my classroom.

But in Finland, when that first week of school arrived, I noticed something odd. Many of my Finnish colleagues hadn't visited their classrooms all summer long. The day before school began, I met one young teacher who admitted she was still deciding what to do that week. I was a little shocked. To my American eyes, my highly trained Finnish colleagues didn't look particularly ready or organized for the first days of school. They seemed naively laid-back. Meanwhile, I felt incredibly stressed, as I strived to teach the textbook-perfect way.

During one of my tightly scripted lessons that week, I told my Helsinki fifth graders we would practice the routine of walking in a quiet, straight line—and, immediately, I heard groans. Apparently, my Finnish students had been navigating the hallways on their own since they were first graders, and my plan irked them. Embarrassed, I ditched this task and quickly moved on to another activity.

I had entered that school year thinking that, as long as I controlled the clock and the physical environment, everything would turn out fine in my classroom. But my Finnish colleagues and students challenged this notion. They seemed to prefer to keep things a little loose at the beginning of the year. To understand this philosophy better, I spoke with a handful of Finnish teachers, all of whom had never been taught the "right" way to begin a school year.

"I think it's important to have a 'soft start' in order to let the school routines and procedures gently grow into the kids," said Johanna Hopia, a classroom teacher at Martti Ahtisaari Elementary School in Kuopio, Finland. In Hopia's classroom, the first days are usually spent discussing summer vacation, playing games, and exercising together. During this time, she neither hands out textbooks nor assigns homework. Jere Linnanen, a history teacher at Helsinki's Maunula Comprehensive School, prefers that his students have "an organic process" of returning to school. "I want to start the school with as little stress as possible," Linnanen said, "both for myself and my students." Last August, he and his colleagues took four groups of ninth graders to a nearby park, where they chatted, danced improvisationally, and played soccer, basketball, and Pokémon Go. Linnanen described the first couple of school days as *ryhmäyttäminen*, which literally translates as "grouping" but means something similar to the English term "team building." At my Helsinki public school I found a similar policy, where teachers and students started with a half day and a regular class schedule didn't start until the following week. Even at the high school level in Finland, it's "very common" for students not to have regular classes on their first day back, according to Taru Pohtola, a foreign-language teacher at Martinlaakso High School in the Finnish city of Vantaa. At Pohtola's school, freshmen get an extra day to settle into the new school environment. "We want them to feel more at home at their new school before the real work begins," she said.

During my first days of teaching in Finland, I led my fifth graders to one of our school's gymnasiums for structured, group games during their only recess blocks. I had picked the activities; they followed my rules. But this routine quickly grew boring, mostly because I ran out of fun games to introduce. Thankfully, one of my Finnish students suggested that we play Kick the Can, something my class had played with their fourth grade teacher. I agreed, and the little blond boy returned with an empty plastic soda bottle.

For the next few weeks of school, I played Kick the Can with my Helsinki fifth graders at least once every day. Actually, it was the only group game they wanted to play with me. Moreover, they wanted me to be "it" every time, which meant that I'd count to twenty, they'd hide, and I'd try to find them. Every time I'd spot my fifth graders and call out their names, we'd link arms, creating an amoeba-like force. If I caught every one of my students, I'd win, but alas, that never happened because a sneaky fifth grader would inevitably kick over the soda bottle (with a triumphant shout), freeing all of my prisoners.

Through our wild rounds of Kick the Can, I saw that the most valuable thing I could do during those early days of school was relax—like my laid-back Finnish colleagues—and simply enjoy relationships with my students. I think I've known for a while that strengthening relationships is very important, especially in the beginning of the year. But one of the obstacles I faced was the pressure to do everything right, from the start.

Many of the Finnish educators I spoke with recognized that classroom structure, which typically stems from establishing rules, routines, and procedures, is valuable, but they emphasized the importance of fostering a welcoming, low-stress learning environment first. While many American schools may lack the slow-start schedule that many Finnish schools implement, I think we can start slow in our classrooms, in order to nurture relationships and a laid-back atmosphere, to lay the groundwork for a great year of learning.

One of the best things I can do with my students, at the beginning of the school year, is simply play with them. It's something that calms those jitters on the first days of school and develops our sense of camaraderie.

My favorite classroom game to play on the first day of school is human bingo. What I love about the game is that it's a fun, active, zero-stress way of strengthening relationships—and it's an activity that can work at any grade level. While the rules of human bingo vary, I'll tell you the simple way I've learned to play the game (Ferlazzo, 2016).

Each student (and teacher) receives a bingo card, but instead of numbers each square contains short descriptions, such as "I've traveled to Europe" or "I've ridden a horse." Then a timer is set for ten or fifteen minutes, and the players circulate around the classroom with their cards in an effort to check off as many bingo squares as possible before the time expires.

Each player works like a social scientist and treats their bingo card like a survey. In order to check off as many bingo squares as possible, players must ask one another questions that correspond with descriptions on their cards, such as "Have you traveled to Europe?" or "Have you ridden a horse?" Once a player finds another player who matches a bingo square description, the square can be checked-off with that player's signature. Before playing, I give my students two rules. First, you can't sign your own card, even if you match some of the descriptions. Second, you can collect only one signature from each player.

After the time expires, I've found that it's valuable to debrief the experience. First, I recognize the effort of the students by asking a series of progress-related questions, such as, "Anyone find more than one match? More than two matches?" and so on until there are no longer any hands raised in the air. Second, if there's time, I'd ask my students to reflect briefly on what they learned about one another: "Did anything surprise you?"

While it's easy to find ready-to-print human bingo cards through Google, I prefer to make my own in a spreadsheet, allowing me to make something perfectly tailored to my students. Because human bingo is one of the first things I do with my students, I want to make a great first impression. In Finland, for example, I wouldn't use a card with the description "I've traveled to Europe," but I might use "I've traveled to America." And if I'm playing the game with beginning readers (kindergartners, first graders, and second graders), I'd probably choose to substitute simple pictures for word-based descriptions, which I can briefly preteach before the game begins.

While I appreciate structured games, like Human Bingo, I think there's also a need for students to feel ownership, right from the start of the school year, and choose their favorite games to play with their teachers, like my fifth graders who called for Kick the Can. I recommend joining your kids on the playground during the first few days of school. I don't think it's necessary to "lead" any games; rather, I suggest that you join the children in their play. If you're a middle school or high school teacher, how about the idea of coordinating a fun, low-key get-together during that first week of school, like Jere Linnanen and his colleagues did with four groups of ninth graders?

Celebrate their learning

During my two years of teaching at a Finnish public school, I found myself very interested in the subjects I'd never seen taught in American public schools, specifically home economics ("cooking class"), textiles, and woodworking. And on several occasions, during my free time I'd sneak into my colleagues' classrooms to get an inside look.

Once, I visited the home economics classroom—a large room with several kitchenettes and dining tables in front of the teacher's desk—and found that not only were the ninth grade students learning how to cook, but also they were given time to enjoy their work, time to celebrate their learning.

The classroom celebration looked simple, but I thought it was the most appropriate way to honor the students' efforts in home economics. The teacher reserved the last fifteen to twenty minutes of the lesson for these ninth graders to enjoy the food they made. After this initial visit, I returned several more times to the home economics classroom, and I continued to see the same thing. There always seemed to be time for students to savor their edible creations.

This simple practice, I argue, promoted their achievement and their autonomy in the classroom, but it also benefited their sense of belonging—the teacher and the students pursued a challenging goal *together*, and then they celebrated their finished work *together*.

Before sitting down to dine at the tables, they needed to complete several tasks in a limited amount of time: food preparation, cleaning the kitchenettes, filling the dish-washer, doing the laundry, and setting the tables with dishes, cups, and flatware. Remembering myself as a teen-age boy, I had a hard time imagining that I would have ever taken a cooking class seriously, but when I looked around the classroom, on every occasion I saw girls *and* boys work-ing carefully to prepare tasty dishes and manage all of the other required tasks.

In that classroom, it seemed clear to me that these hard-working students were developing into competent cooks because they were intrinsically motivated. I didn't see them pushing themselves to cook well because they wanted to please their teacher or pad their GPAs. They cooked well, I deduced, because the process was enjoyable (three ingredi-ents of happiness, by the way, were on full display: belong-ing, autonomy, and mastery), and they had adequate time to enjoy their food at the end of class. Without those final fif-teen to twenty minutes of celebrating, I doubt that they would have worked with the same level of concentration and enjoyment.

In my work as a writer I've experienced a similar phe-nomenon. The moment I see my writing published, the hours I poured into the process feel worthwhile and I derive great satisfaction from having a little time to stop and cele-brate the achievement. I can't imagine if I was forced to keep producing words without stopping to feel grateful for my labor. In my work as a teacher, on the other hand, I admit that it has been harder for me to experience those moments of healthy pride. But I wonder if that's because, historically speaking, I've rarely made it a point to celebrate my students' learning.

The first step requires that we stop seeing a celebration of learning as an unneeded add-on and start seeing it as something that brings meaning to the students' work, motivates them to learn more effectively, and promotes a learning community. A celebration might take fifteen or twenty minutes of an occasional lesson, as it does in a Finnish home economics classroom, but imagine the benefits of this (relatively) small investment.

One thing I tried with my Helsinki students was "book talks." The practice was simple: I'd work with my students to choose appropriately leveled books, they'd prepare little reports showing their understanding of the texts, and then they'd give five-minute presentations (book talks) in front of their classmates.

Initially I didn't conceive of book talks as a celebration of learning, but after two rounds of them during my students' sixth grade year, it appeared to achieve this result. I received feedback from several students telling me how much they enjoyed the opportunity to speak to their classmates about their books and hear their classmates talk about their books. Also, I heard several of my sixth graders say out loud, during presentations, how badly they wanted to get their hands on particular books being discussed. I remember seeing, at least once, a student lending her classmate the book she had just described in her presentation. My students were inspiring one another to learn more, which was something that brought me a lot of joy.

Reserving time for my students to publicly present their learning gave their work—reading their books carefully and writing insightful reports—greater purpose. Many of my students saw their book talks as opportunities to recommend their books to their classmates, or warn them in advance. Perhaps my favorite part about book talks was that it seemed to bring our classroom closer together as learners. My students were teaching and learning from one another, and that element of celebrating their work seemed to strengthen their sense of belonging.

Here are some other ideas for celebrating the learning:

- You can reserve a few minutes, at the end of a writing lesson, to have several students read their pieces (such as stories or poems) to the class. During my last year of teaching in Boston, I implemented this routine in our writer's workshop, and my first and second graders loved it—it brought them closer together as learners and motivated them to produce higher-quality drafts during class.
- Your classroom could host an evening for the school community, in which they exhibit their work. While I've seen large exhibition nights at schools, which tend to require many hours on behalf of students and teachers, I think smaller-scale productions can work well, too. In her 2002 book *Reading With Meaning*, American teacher Debbie Miller describes her first grade classroom's Coffeehouse Poetry Day:

The muted trumpet of Miles Davis plays on the CD player, floating among the voices in the crowded classroom. Hot chocolate simmers in the PTA's relic of a coffeepot; a mountain of miniature marshmallows fills a bowl nearby. Long rolls of deep blue paper decorated with . . . crescent moons cover the windows and darken the room. Table lamps and tiny white lights draped from the ceiling provide the only light.

Freshly scrubbed tables are rearranged into cozy groups of two. Handmade flowers in tiny clay pots, poetry books, bowls of pretzels, and small containers of words from magnetic poetry kits have replaced crayons, markers, scissors, sticky notes, pencils, and glue.

Parents and children sit together, munching pretzels and sipping steamy hot chocolate in mugs brought from home, reading poetry by the likes of Eloise Greenfield, Maya Angelou, Aileen Fisher, Jane Yolen, Valerie Worth, and Georgia Heard. But the poems receiving the most enthusiastic reviews? They're the ones written by the children themselves, published and bound into books with enough copies for everyone. (p. 74)

- To celebrate the learning of your students, you can set up a class blog. While this initiative could work well for any age group, I think it's especially meaningful to older students, who have the possibility of sharing ownership with the teacher.

In the simplest terms, a good celebration of learning is a pause to give thanks, communally, for the good work of the children.

Pursue a class dream

Camp School is a huge celebration of learning in Finland

because it's something that comes at the end of the children's elementary school career. Students anticipate Camp School for years, and many classrooms start raising money months in advance. There are two major reasons that I appreciate this Finnish practice.

First of all, I admire how much responsibility is expected from students to raise money for this sleepaway excursion. The amount needed for everyone to attend Camp School is significant, often totaling thousands of euros, so fundraising should start well before the trip through different student-led initiatives, such as hosting bake sales and school dances.

Second, pursuing a class dream, by raising a large sum of money *and* attending Camp School together, promotes a strong sense of classroom unity. My Finnish colleague, who also taught a sixth grade classroom the same year I did, had Camp School early in the fall, and when she and her students returned to school, I remember noticing a positive change in their rapport.

In the spring of that school year, I saw a similar phenomenon with my group of sixth graders. After returning from Camp School, my students looked more like a team than a group of twenty-four individuals. The trip proved to be a powerful bonding experience. My only regret was that it didn't happen earlier in my two-year journey with my class.

But my experience in Finland got me thinking about how important a major social-bonding experience like Camp School is for promoting connectedness in the classroom. And because belonging is a crucial ingredient of happiness (and any joyful classroom), I recommend that teachers pursue similar class dreams.

Finnish-style Camp School is great, but it requires a significant investment of time and money, so it may not be a good fit for you and your students. But, thankfully, there are many other class dreams to be realized. What if the dream was to produce a music album, with songs written and played by the students? Or hiking up a mountain? Or creating a learning app? The possibilities are endless.

So how could a class go about pursuing a class dream? First, the teacher and students need to make a decision *together.* As teachers, many of us would be tempted to predetermine the dream for our class. During my first year of teaching in Finland, I made the mistake of deciding on a class dream, without consulting my students. Before the school year began, actually, I had already committed to a particular vision. I imagined an interdisciplinary project I found exciting, service oriented, and motivating for my students. I decided that we would raise money for a good cause by financially supporting young Finnish Paralympians while raising consciousness about the (relative) lack of funding they receive as handicapped athletes. I envisioned that my class would conduct several interviews with these athletes, write about their experiences on their student blogs, and possibly start a national conversation in Finland! Even before meeting my Helsinki students, I arranged classroom visits from Finnish Paralympians, and I felt confident that my fifth graders, whom I didn't know personally, would share my enthusiasm.

In hindsight, this class dream seemed destined to fail, because if it was going to be *our* dream, I needed to make the decision *with* my students.

During those first weeks of school, my Helsinki fifth graders seemed inspired by particular aspects of this project, especially the classroom visits with Paralympians, but they didn't appear to catch my vision. For example, I thought it would be meaningful to raise a lot of money for these handicapped athletes, but some of my students voiced understandable concerns. They wondered how they could achieve this additional fundraising goal, because they planned to raise a lot of money for Camp School.

As the early weeks of school passed by, it became increasingly clear to me this class dream wasn't going to work. It wasn't a shared vision, and it wasn't realistic. And I felt quite discouraged. I decided that it would be best to scrap the project and simply move on. Although this early failure in Finland wasn't pleasant, it taught me a lot about the value of including students in the planning process and the importance of deciding on a reasonable dream. Thankfully, I felt like my initial mistake of choosing a class dream was redeemed as my students and I pursued and enjoyed Camp School as a shared aspiration.

Once you've decided on a realistic dream *with* your students, I think it's important to start by discussing roles. For Camp School, my students were primarily responsible for fundraising while I supported them by supervising their progress. I'd allow them to meet in our classroom during fifteen-minute breaks to plan, and during their fundraisers (bake sales and school dances) I'd make myself available to them. However, I wouldn't do the actual work of fundraising, because that was viewed as the work of the children. This philosophy, I've found, is something that other teachers, parents, and students in Finland appear to share.

Behind the scenes, I did what would have been challenging for my young students, for example, working with a parent liaison to pay for our class trip. This parent opened a Camp School bank account where the money for the trip would be deposited. After fundraisers, my students would count the money—in math class, typically—and then I'd lock up the money until the parent representative was ready to pick up the cash. Later, the parent would pay the expenses of the trip, through the class bank account. Throughout the process, I worked together with the parent liaison to communicate with other parents in the class. One of my jobs was to make reservations for the trip. We needed food, lodging, and a bus. And, after hearing about my colleague's positive experience at Camp School, I started to plan that we would have our trip at the same location. I assumed that my students would be happy with the idea of attending the same Camp School as the classroom next door. I was mistaken.

Many wanted to stay at a different venue, even after hearing that I had already made a reservation at another Camp School site. That was a little upsetting, but I felt like I knew what to do: we'd vote on those two options, and whichever option fetched the most votes would be our choice. The overwhelming majority of my sixth graders voted to attend the other Camp School site, the one I *hadn't* reserved. So I canceled the first reservation, and made a new reservation based on my students' selection. Ultimately, this change brought joy to my students, and that brought me joy, even if it required a little extra work. We also voted on which activities we'd participate in as a class, before leaving for our sports-themed Camp School.

When negotiating a class dream, teachers and students

will probably need to make compromises, but that democratic process brings a classroom closer together. At Camp
School, we had the pleasure of doing so many fun activities
together in a just a few days, like Ultimate Frisbee, flag foot-
ball, archery, swimming, and a mini Olympics.

One evening we reserved a sauna by a little pond, where
the water was frigid (anyone who dove into it would scream,
including me). Another night we reserved a campsite by a
lake, where we roasted marshmallows and ate pancakes with
strawberry jam as the sun was setting. That night I tried
teaching my students how to skip stones, but when I demonstrated, I slid into the lake, completely drenching one of my
sneakers. We all laughed about this for a long time.

After the trip, we had a reflection session in our classroom, and I was impressed with how many joyful, memora-
ble experiences we had shared together in such a short span
of time. Camp School felt like the most perfect way to end
our two years together. I was left feeling, too, that something like Camp School would have been a perfect way to
begin our journey as a class.

One downside of our Camp School trip was the absence of
a few members of our class. For personal reasons, several
students decided to stay back, where they joined my colleague's classroom for a handful of days. I respected their
choice—at the same time, I wished they could have shared
those memories with us. When we returned, I suspected
they might have felt a little left out as many students fondly
recalled Camp School.

For teachers who want to pursue a class dream with their
students, I think it's important to keep this point in mind: a
powerful group experience like Camp School is meaningful

only to those who participate. Students who sit out won't achieve the same sense of belonging as the other children. So it's wise, in my opinion, to cast a vision with your students that promotes the involvement of *everyone*.

I was very pleased with our class dream, but it was *not* something I, the teacher, could have accomplished on my own. Everyone connected with our class played a role: other teachers, students, and their parents. I highly recommend finding another teacher who can offer advice and join your project. Perhaps you can be that supportive teacher for a colleague, too.

For our Camp School, I was incredibly grateful to have a veteran colleague join our class for those three days, and before coming, she insisted on serving our class in ways I didn't expect: she called to confirm our reservation, purchased groceries for our cookouts, and arranged a meeting with me to go over an important Camp School checklist. (During the trip she even made pancake batter with a couple of my sixth grade boys!) My colleague gave our class a big gift, and that service not only made our trip operate smoothly, with much less stress on my part, but also brought me a lot of joy, knowing that another teacher was equally invested. While sharing Camp School with another teacher, I think it was easier for me to focus on *enjoying* the experience rather than managing the experience.

Class dreams can be as big as teachers and students make them, but the most important thing to remember is that they should be *shared* and *realistic*.

Banish the bullying

As the leaders of our classrooms, there's a lot we can do to discourage bullying—or, in other words, stop it before it starts. The strategies I've mentioned so far in this chapter—*know each child, play with your students, celebrate their learning,* and *pursue a class dream*—support this goal. By strengthening the sense of belonging in our classroom, they serve as preventive measures. But sometimes, despite our best efforts to promote positive interactions in our classroom, behavior that looks and sounds like bullying can happen. And when it does, we need an approach for addressing it immediately.

From 18 percent to 31 percent of America's kids and adolescents experience school-based bullying, according to a report from the U.S. National Academies of Sciences, Engineering, and Medicine. While definitions of bullying vary, notes reporter Roxanne Khamsi (2016), "the most common way to define the behavior seems to be as repeated intentional and aggressive actions in which the perpetrator has greater power—regardless of whether that power imbalance is real or simply perceived."

While living in the United States, I taught in three American schools (two public and one private), and in each one I found sensible ways for stopping bullying before it starts. I remember seeing morning circles, regular whole-school gatherings, an antibullying workshop, and a huge poster that was signed by students as a pledge to stand up to bullying. Those seemed like good preventive measures, but the one thing I didn't see was a school-wide system for addressing bullying-like behavior.

For more than a decade, Finland has been seeking to address the problem of bullying in its schools. And at my Helsinki school, I was introduced to the nation's most popu-

lar antibullying program, called KiVa, which is now implemented in 90 percent of Finland's schools. KiVa is an
abbreviation of the Finnish words *kiusaamista vastaan*, meaning "against bullying." It's also wordplay, because the word
kiva translates as "nice" (Khamsi, 2016).

This nationwide antibullying program appears promising. In a study of seven thousand students in Finnish schools,
researchers found that KiVa significantly improved the mental health of children suffering from the highest frequency of
bullying (Ring, 2016).

There are preventive components of KiVa's strategy:
students receive instruction about bullying (with the help
of computer software, for example), and they role-play in
the classroom (Ring, 2016). As I taught in Helsinki, I saw
another valuable aspect of the program: a clear set of steps
to follow when bullying appears to happen. (To recall
KiVa's protocol, I spoke with my former Helsinki colleague,
Paula Havu, who attended training sessions for this antibullying program.)

Let's say there's a conflict between several students. One
child accuses a few classmates of something that appears
bullyish, like regularly being left out of games on the playground. Those students can request a KiVa meeting by
speaking with a teacher. (This process can also be initiated
by bystanders, such as teachers and classmates who observed
the bullying-like behavior.) Then the teacher, with those students, completes a form, briefly describing the incident, and
agrees upon a negotiation date and place. Then the teacher
puts this completed form in a special folder, monitored regularly by a team of KiVa teachers, who then communicate
with a team of older students, who have been trained to

address these conflicts. This way these older students can attend and facilitate these negotiations.

At this conflict resolution session, typically in an unused classroom during a break, the teacher, the two parties, and the older students meet together. During this KiVa conflict resolution session, both parties tell their respective sides of the story. The initial focus is on listening to one another. Next, the facilitators ask each party to reflect on their behavior, thinking about how they could have acted differently. The idea is that these students will identify possible solutions for preventing this situation. Once each side promises to implement a preventive strategy, which is written down by the KiVa facilitators, the meeting is finished.

"In KiVa, you don't need to say sorry unless you want to," said Paula Havu. "Because, usually, when you are told to say sorry you don't necessarily mean it. . . . In KiVa, you try to focus on where the problem is and how you behaved and how you could have behaved differently." Usually, a follow-up meeting is scheduled with these two parties, two weeks into the future, when the conflict is revisited. If the problem persists, additional protocol is followed and parents are notified.

Bullying in Finnish schools isn't tolerated, but the idea behind the KiVa program is that there are lots of (relatively) small actions, such as holding conflict resolution talks or role-playing situations in the classroom, that can be taken to prevent bullying from happening. "It's a really good program," my colleague Paula assured me.

While I taught in American schools, I think my students and I would have benefited from implementing several key elements of the KiVa program. In hindsight, bullying-type behavior would sometimes flare up in my classroom, but I wasn't sure how to address it. Having ongoing discussions with my students about bullying and how to stand up against it would have been useful.

Also, I think it would have been important for me to establish a system for addressing the complaints of my students. Usually, I'd address conflicts only when I saw them spilling over. Perhaps I could have left a mailbox in the classroom, like the KiVa folder in Finnish schools, for my students to inform me about difficult interactions with one another.

Lastly, I think I could have emphasized solutions, more than "sorrys," whenever conflicts would spring up in my American classroom. Typically, I'd nudge my young students to apologize before putting the situation behind us, but I rarely dwelled on the positive actions my students could have taken. Writing down their forward-thinking solutions and scheduling a follow-up meeting with them would have been wise, too.

Bullying in our schools is an obvious joy destroyer, but so too are the small steps that students take toward that sad outcome. Thankfully, the KiVa program suggests different ways that we can protect the joy in our classroom by helping students take ownership for standing up to bullying.

Buddy up

At my Helsinki school, I noticed a unique tradition in which the sixth grade classrooms would team up with first grade classrooms. Initially I admired the practice from a distance, but when my fifth graders turned into sixth graders I got to experience this approach with my class firsthand.

That fall my class visited the first grade classroom, where

my students were assigned to buddy up with the youngest members of our school. I remember our collaboration started with a scavenger hunt throughout the school, prepared by the first grade teacher. And from that day forward, this buddy system seemed to boost the first graders' sense of belonging at school. On the playground, during those fifteen-minute breaks, I'd see first graders tagging along with my students and hugging them incessantly. (At times the affection of some little ones became so intense that I'd need to intervene and rescue my sixth graders—they'd thank me.)

Throughout that school year, my class teamed up with the first grade class in different ways. We had at least a couple of lessons together, where my students assisted them with their schoolwork. Also, we did fieldwork together on at least one occasion. The arrangement was modest, requiring little additional prep and communication, but I think this practice contributed to a higher level of belonging in our school, especially for the first graders. I'd argue, too, that my sixth graders had a greater sense of purpose at school because of the buddy system. I sensed that many of my students could see that their kindness to our school's youngest members made a difference.

The buddy system is not a mandated practice in Finnish schools, or even a widespread one, in my understanding, but through experiencing this tradition at my Helsinki school I saw how well this approach can boost a sense of belonging in the school setting. Paula Havu, my former colleague and the teacher of the first grade class I'd sometimes observe during my first year in Helsinki, told me more about her experiences with the buddy system:

With my twenty-eight kids in the classroom, including "integrated" kids, we were still able to go to so many places because of the buddy system, because I had [the sixth grade teacher] and the sixth graders with us. I knew that every single kid would have an older student to stand next to. And those older students, although they're kind of teenagers, when they are given responsibility, when they are trusted, [when] they get a little buddy to walk with them . . . they change. They don't need to be tough. They don't need to be cool. They need to take care of that little guy over there and be [the role model].

Paula has an interesting theory for why the buddy system seems to work well:

Sometimes, the class has certain dynamics and students have certain roles in the classroom. But then when you mix it up with another classroom, those group dynamics change. And you don't have to necessarily be that tough guy in your own classroom—you can actually be part of the different group.

During our phone conversation, I told Paula that many teachers in the United States feel like they lack time for teaming up with colleagues, because they're too busy and stressed out. "But part of that," Paula interrupted me, "is also that you do [develop] stress when you have to do everything on your own. The moment you share it with someone else, it becomes easier."

While pairing sixth graders with first graders seems

sensible, I think other arrangements could work well, too. Why not pair an eighth grade class with a sixth grade class? Or a second grade class with a kindergarten class? Even children close in age can reap the benefits of buddying up with each other.

As I suggested before, the *buddy up* strategy is reasonably low prep. What's essential is that this kind of bond between your classroom and another classroom is established early in the school year, so that students (and teachers) can enjoy that heightened sense of belonging throughout that year.

CHAPTER
3
Autonomy

IN MY FIRST YEAR OF TEACHING IN FINLAND, THE day before the first day of school, there was a faculty meeting in the teachers' lounge, and my principal asked—before dismissing everyone—if there were any questions. I still had many, but a specific one continued to burn in my mind: where would I escort my fifth graders when the school day would end?

In America, at every elementary school I had ever visited, at the end of each school day teachers would lead their students to the exits, where the children would either ride the bus or get picked up by an adult (or, in very rare cases, walk home). I assumed there was a similar protocol in Helsinki.

But when I posed this question to the faculty, my colleagues looked baffled.

In hindsight, their confusion made perfect sense. That's because my fellow Helsinki teachers *weren't* typically escorting their students to the exits. Their kids would simply leave the classroom, exiting the school on their own—even the first graders.

So the next day I did what my Finnish colleagues were in the habit of doing. When my last lesson concluded, I dismissed my fifth graders without leading them to the exits and, out of curiosity, I watched them fetch their backpacks from the coat rack in the hallway. Several of my students took out their own cell phones and called their parents, which was a totally unfamiliar sight for me. Not only that, but I overheard some of them telling their parents they were heading home—on their own.

Later, I casually surveyed my fifth graders on this subject, and I saw three-fourths of my class raise their hands to say they were commuting on their own. I'd eventually learn that some took the subway, a few took the tram, and others walked and biked.

That same school year, I met a second grade girl who told me that she'd walk home alone. (It was about one kilometer away, through the center of Finland's capital city.) She told me that often no one else was home when she arrived at her family's apartment, but instead of twiddling her thumbs, she'd complete her homework (if she had any) and fix herself a snack. Fried eggs were her favorite. When I told a couple of my fifth graders about this little girl, their attitude was like, "No big deal, man." One of my students claimed he had been commuting home alone since preschool—and I remember thinking, *What planet am I on?*

Generally, Finnish children seem much more autonomous than American kids, but they don't possess an independence gene, of course. What they have, I've observed, are many opportunities, at home and at school, to do things by themselves without handholding, and through those opportunities, they seem more self-directed as learners.

As a teacher in the United States, I had always tried to develop autonomy in my students, especially in the beginning of the school year, but in Finland, where I found that many of my fifth graders were already fiercely independent, I was challenged to rethink my teaching practices. Academic literature suggests that a sense of autonomy is a major ingredient of happiness (Pinsker, 2016), and during those two years of teaching in Helsinki I saw that, too—my students seemed to thrive whenever I would make decisions to develop their agency.

In an interview with a group of Finnish kindergarten educators at Niirala Preschool in Kuopio, I asked them about the best ways to promote joy in the classroom, and the second element they suggested—after good teacher–student relationships (a sense of belonging)—was opportunities for children to impact the classroom. They, too, had identified a link between joy and autonomy. In Finland's latest curriculum reform, developing student agency, inside and outside of school, is one of the major emphases, along with prioritizing the joy of learning and cultivating a collaborative learning environment (Halinen, 2015).

As a teacher, promoting the autonomy of students is something that I view as incredibly important, but I admit, humbly, that it's an area of my craft I still need to prioritize and cultivate. That being said, through working with super-independent children in Finland, I've identified several teaching strategies that develop student agency.

Start with freedom

In my graduate training as a teacher, I had always heard that scaffolding was a wise thing to do. Specifically, I held onto one theory: the gradual release of responsibility, which suggests that we teachers limit the autonomy of students until we see that our children are ready for greater freedom. For years I worked hard to maintain a tight grip on classroom activities, from the very beginning of a particular learning experience.

But when I started teaching in Helsinki, somehow this philosophy of the gradual release of responsibility didn't feel right anymore—my fifth graders already seemed so capable, and when given freedom outside of the classroom, they appeared to thrive. I began to wonder if the philosophy of gradually releasing responsibility could be more effective if it was flipped around: what if, instead of starting with significant restriction in my classroom, I started with significant freedom? My breakthrough moment occurred several weeks into the school year.

For Camp School fundraising, my fifth graders wanted to host a bake sale during the school day. Honestly, I didn't like the idea at first, because it sounded like another responsibility for me to manage. But my students insisted they could arrange the event without my help. So I gave them the green light, and they surprised me. My fifth graders created advertisements, managed a class sign-up form, carried in loads of baked goods, set up furniture, and priced all of the treats. All of these things were completed without my direction. I made myself available through supervising my students, but I didn't hold their hands throughout the process. That first bake sale was a success in my mind not only because my class raised a large sum of money for Camp School but also because they had demonstrated what they could accomplish individually and collectively, when provided with a greater degree of autonomy.

Later that first year, the other fifth grade teacher and I experimented by offering an "Independent Learning Week." (Several of my students' subject teachers participated, too.) At the beginning of this week, we provided our students with a list of tasks to complete in nearly every academic subject. And we told them that we wouldn't have regular lessons for the next few days. Instead, they would have open blocks where they could finish these tasks at their own pace. We trusted them to reach out to us when they needed help.

During Independent Learning Week, we weren't circulating around the classroom and peering over their shoulders. Instead, we provided our students with opportunities to wrestle with their work first. My grade-level partner and I were trusting our fifth graders with a significant amount of instructional time—nearly fifteen hours' worth—and yet, surprisingly, I didn't feel anxious. From the bake sale experience and other occasions, I knew my students were capable of being successful while having a large degree of autonomy. Ultimately, my students continued to impress me. All the children finished their work, even if they needed extra time.

In America, I've heard teachers discuss the importance of

evolving from the traditional model of the "sage on the stage" who transmits knowledge to students to the "guide on the side" who stands back, encourages students to construct meaning, and offers coaching along the way. I think there's wisdom in this latter approach, but the strategy I'm suggesting here, *start with freedom,* differs slightly.

Based on my experiences in Finland, I'm recommending we teachers provide children with more low-stakes opportunities to approach their learning. Over those two years, I kept finding that my Helsinki students would rise to the occasion, surprising me with what they could already do on their own.

Start with freedom, in a parallel way, is similar to the practice of a pretest (an assessment administered before instruction), in which students have an opportunity to demonstrate what they already know during the early stage of learning. Pretesting is a wise practice because, when designed well, it can inform teachers about appropriate starting points for instruction. It paves the way for more efficient teaching.

Before moving to Finland, I used to be wary of giving my students greater autonomy in the beginning of a school year, classroom activity, or project, because I feared that they'd get off track without my handholding, but nowadays, I think it makes sense to begin with freedom, because it allows me to see what the children are *already* capable of doing, just like a good pretest.

In the classroom, sometimes children want to do things we suspect are too hard for them to accomplish independently, like reading a book beyond their reading level or solving an incredibly complicated math problem. During these occasions, we basically have two options as teachers:

we can either let them dive into those challenges or steer them away. In my teaching experiences, stretching back to my time in American schools, my students have looked encouraged whenever I've given them the green light, signaling that I believe in their capabilities, even if I can foresee the potential pitfalls. If my students fail to do the challenging things they hope to accomplish, no harm done. At least they've proven to themselves that they weren't ready, quite yet. And at this point in the learning process, it's likely that they're more open to my guidance.

During my second year of teaching in Finland, I received an e-mail from one of my students who suggested that we incorporate a quiz website called Kahoot! in our classroom. He provided a brief testimonial saying he had used the website outside of school and loved it. Initially I was skeptical of this idea, just as I had been when my Helsinki students told me they wanted to host a bake sale. My first thought was that a quiz website would raise the level of competition among students, which was something I wanted to avoid completely. Not only that, but when I received this e-mail, I felt like I didn't have the bandwidth to learn a new program like Kahoot!

But in my reply, I didn't provide a flat-out no to my student. I told this sixth grader that we should discuss this idea in ethics class. (Ethics, by the way, is a subject in Finland, which can be taken in lieu of a religion class, such as Islam or Lutheran Christianity, in grades one to nine.) With this student and his classmates, I wanted to explore the ethical implications of using a quiz website, which engages in ranking students.

During this classroom conversation about Kahoot!, we

agreed that the best way to discern the appropriateness of this quiz website would be to test it out—and this is where I saw my students rise to the occasion again. Led by the student who e-mailed me, several of my sixth graders independently designed a Kahoot! quiz, which posed questions coinciding with the content of an ethics unit. Later, I'd see for myself that the setup was low maintenance, but my students' ownership, at the time, made such a difference.

When we finally tested out the quiz with the other students in ethics class, the excitement in our classroom was palpable. My sixth graders, who owned smartphones, used their devices to participate in the quiz, working either alone or with partners. Not only did we have a lot of fun answering those multiple-choice questions, as suspenseful music played in the background, but I think everyone was inspired that this playful assessment was designed not by me but by *them*, the students.

If I had dismissed my enthusiastic sixth grader's idea over e-mail, I doubt I would have discovered this fun classroom tool, and most important, I would have missed seeing what he and his classmates were capable of doing on their own. For me, it was yet another anchor lesson, where I witnessed the value of letting go of control and inviting my students to take on more responsibility, from the start.

Leave margin

After a year with my Helsinki students, I decided to restructure many of our language arts lessons. I wanted my sixth graders to spend the majority of class time working on writing projects, which would require them to research, draft, rewrite, edit, and conference with one another and with me. I figured that if they were going to blossom into effective writers, they needed to have lots of opportunities to work like them.

That year we spent many class periods in one of our school's computer labs, which was adjacent to the library. At the beginning of a new writing assignment, I'd provide them with a project description sheet, and after discussing it together, I'd let them work independently. We created a section on the chalkboard where my sixth graders could write down their names as a way to request meetings with me (Ferlazzo, in press), and I could use the same system to request meetings with them. Typically, during a writing conference, a student and I would talk over written comments I had made on their piece of writing, and we'd agree on next steps.

Once I implemented this new framework during language arts, I noticed a positive change almost immediately: I was spending much more time giving constructive feedback to my sixth graders, while my students were spending much more time working on demanding writing projects (Ferlazzo, in press). During these blocks, it was common for my sixth graders to be at different places in their writing: some were brainstorming in their notebooks, some were conferencing at the tables in the middle of the lab, some were drafting at the computers, and some were reading in the library. I didn't mind where my students were in this process, as long as they were focused on their work. Several of my students asked if they could listen to their MP3 players in class, provided they remained on task, and I said sure.

But the new arrangement wasn't all smooth sailing. Some

of my sixth graders seemed to respond perfectly to the self-directed nature of this workshop approach, completing pieces of writing that far surpassed my initial expectations for them. (These were the same students who would eventually develop the habit of giving and receiving detailed feedback from one another, without my encouragement.) But there were other students who appeared to need more direction during these open writing blocks, and it was at this point where I saw the importance of the strategy *leave margin.*

In my first few years of teaching, I'd rarely design lessons with margin—I'd aim to script things so tightly that an off-task student (or some other interruption) could easily high-jack my lesson. It was in Finland that I firmly grasped the value of leaving margin, or flexible time, throughout the school day, when important tweaks could be made to teaching and learning.

In Finnish schools, where frequent fifteen-minute breaks throughout the day are the norm, experiencing margin was natural. If a child in my classroom wanted clarification on an assignment, we could discuss their work during one of those recesses, or if there was a misunderstanding among several of my students, we could troubleshoot during a fifteen-minute respite. Having a schedule in Finland that allowed me to meet with my students, as needed, throughout the day was incredibly helpful. Thankfully, this kind of timetable isn't the only way to accommodate flexible time in a classroom.

As teachers, we can build margin into our lessons. It's something I saw clearly when I changed the format of my language arts lessons. Under the new arrangement, I was glad to see that many of my students were thriving as writers, but there were some who seemed lost. Initially, I remember seeing computer screens with just a few words after forty-five minutes of work, or I'd hear chatter coming from the library, where students were generally expected to read silently. Initially, the workshop approach wasn't working well for everyone, and interventions were needed.

Those fifteen-minute breaks after lessons were useful for conferencing with my sixth graders, but I found that it was most essential to have margin *during* lessons. It was a waste of instructional time if I'd intervene only *after* a forty-five-minute class period. My students needed immediate feedback, especially the ones who were struggling. Thankfully, the structure of the workshop framework allowed for this practice.

Because my students were working independently, I had lots of flexibility in my teaching. I could conference with an individual student, meet with a small group, or circulate around the classroom, checking in quickly with my sixth graders. Providing the children with more autonomy provided me with more autonomy, too.

During those writing workshops, I'd want to conference with students as soon as possible, because these meetings often seemed to be the most beneficial for my students. However, it didn't make sense to start conferences until all of my sixth graders were settled and focused on their work. So I'd usually devote the first few minutes of class to a somewhat slow start, where I could address such issues as forgotten notebooks or a shortage of school computers, as students resumed their writing projects. Once everyone seemed settled, I'd start meeting with individual students, based on the requests written on the chalkboard.

But sometimes, even after I had addressed those initial trouble spots, some students still needed further direction. If I noticed, for example, that a child was spending a significant amount of time scrolling through her MP3 player instead of working, I knew it was a good time to intervene. Ideally, I'd finish a conference and, before inviting another student for a meeting, I'd provide feedback to a student in need.

During my second year of teaching in Finland, the writing workshop model I implemented wasn't perfect, but it provided many more opportunities—for my students and for me—to work autonomously, with plenty of margin along the way. Teachers who want to build in leeway don't need to institute the workshop model (although it's definitely worth considering). What's essential is that students have lots of time to do meaningful independent work, which allows teachers plenty of chances to offer meaningful feedback.

One of the most important times to build in margin is the first lesson of the day. In my experience, children thrive with a few minutes to settle into the school day before turning their attention to today's lessons. In my experience, it's useful to write an age-appropriate message to your students, which my students will read as soon as they enter the classroom (after I greet them, of course!). Then, my students will know to complete worthwhile independent work for about five minutes, such as reading an interesting, appropriately leveled book or practicing math facts. When my students have mastered this routine (through adequate rehearsal and coaching from me), it's something that provides my classroom with a few precious minutes of margin. With this system, I can easily check in with my students—about their homework, about their health, about anything really—as they slowly settle into another day of school.

In fact, I've found that this routine can be implemented effectively *whenever* students enter the classroom, to provide margin and a smooth start to any lesson. In his 2015 book *Teach Like a Champion 2.0*, Doug Lemov calls this a "Do Now" and "the first step in a great lesson" (p. 161). He defines a Do Now as "a short activity that you have written on the board or that, in printed form, is waiting for students as they enter. Either way, the *Do Now* starts working before you do" (p. 161). In *Teach Like a Champion*, Lemov identifies four key criteria:

- The directions for a Do Now need to be located in the same spot in the classroom, whether it's on a white board or a sheet of computer paper taped on the wall, so students know exactly where to look when entering.
- Do Now activities should be independent tasks that don't require further instructions by the teacher or conversations among students.
- It's important to keep a Do Now exercise to three to five minutes in length, so that it doesn't take too much time from the primary lesson of the day. Lemov believes that a Do Now activity must be of the pencil-and-paper variety, to make it "more rigorous and more engaging," and something that allows the teacher "to better hold students accountable" (p. 162). (I disagree with him on this point; I've found that giving students time to read great books, for example,

works as a simple, effective Do Now, as long as the
children already have these texts with them.)

- In general, a good Do Now, according to Lemov,
should "preview the day's lesson" or "review a recent
lesson" (p. 162). (These are admirable aims, but I think
it works well, too, if students continue to work on an
independent project immediately, such as a writing
assignment, or, as I mentioned before, dive back into a
great book.)

"The single most common downfall I observe with *Do
Nows*," writes Lemov, "is a teacher's losing track of time
while reviewing answers [to the activity]. Fifteen minutes
later, the *Do Now* has replaced the lesson that was originally
planned" (p. 162). To avoid this, Lemov recommends spending no more than three to five minutes reviewing a Do Now
with your students. This sounds sensible. In my opinion, the
most important reason for implementing a Do Now routine
is to provide a little margin, so that my students and I can
hit the ground running when we dive into the lesson. While
Lemov suggests that we teachers give our students the same
Do Now assignment, I think students are more motivated to
do this work when they're provided with choices. In fact,
students thrive, I've found, whenever they're offered a variety of options.

Offer choices

While the experiment of Independent Learning Week was
successful (in the sense that all of my students completed
their work), it had one major flaw: my Helsinki fifth graders
lacked choices. I could argue that my students had lots of

freedom during Independent Learning Week because they could choose when to complete any given assignment during those fifteen classroom hours. But I don't think that argument would have satisfied many of my fifth graders.

Sitting in a circle on the floor, after completing Independent Learning Week, I heard their feedback loud and clear. Many of my students felt that too much work was assigned, especially in math. Not only that, but some of them also complained that the week's tasks felt irrelevant and boring.

Their feedback was valuable, but I admit that it wasn't nice to hear. I wanted to focus on the positive side (everyone eventually finished the mountain of work!). But what seemed most important to dwell on—to many of my Helsinki fifth graders, at least—was the major flaw they perceived in the Independent Learning Week: a lack of good choices.

I found myself agreeing with their critique. By assigning everyone the *same* boatload of tasks, Independent Learning Week had failed to account for their individual learning strengths and interests. For that reason, my students weren't offered good choices. They were simply following my orders, aligned with the curriculum.

After that experience, I felt reluctant to try Independent Learning Week again. I knew it wasn't a catastrophe—my students had worked autonomously and found success—but I sensed that doing it again (and doing it better) would require a significant shift. If I was going to offer them good choices, I'd need to do a better job of connecting their interests to the curriculum (something I discuss later). In hindsight, most assignments of the Independent Learning Week were rigid and intentionally manageable for both teachers and students, like the task of completing math problems from a workbook. There was little room for students to exercise choice *while* working.

During my meeting with a small group of Finnish kindergarten educators at Niirala Preschool in Kuopio, Finland, they suggested that their primary job, as teachers, is to make the connection between student interests and the curriculum. They explained that, in order to facilitate this convergence, they need to identify the interests of their students first, so observing children and discussing their interests is always a priority in their classrooms. One of these Finnish educators remarked that if a child showed interest in Angry Birds, a teacher could leverage this fascination in the classroom. Initially, it seemed like a stretch of the imagination, but I decided to bite my tongue. At the end of the meeting I asked her about this idea of connecting a child's interest in Angry Birds to the curriculum. I wanted concrete examples. Gleefully, these three kindergarten educators suggested different possibilities: categorizing, counting, naming, story building, role-playing . . . they could have continued to rattle off different curriculum-related exercises, but I playfully shouted, Enough!

Those Finnish kindergarten educators had made it seem incredibly simple: get to know your students' passions, make curricular connections, and then offer interesting choices to them. Although they instruct five-, six-, and seven-year-old children, I think this approach is wise for teachers at all age levels. We need to know the curricula well, as teachers, but we need to know the interests of our students, too, if we're committed to offering meaningful, interesting work in our classrooms. Too often in my teaching, I think I've neglected to identify the interests of *all* of my students—and that's the first step.

One simple way of connecting student interests with the curriculum, I've discovered, is providing tasks that are more open-ended. For example, instead of assigning the same book for everyone to report on, I allowed my Helsinki students to choose their own books of interest and present their learning through a poster, a slideshow, or a website. They'd still need to demonstrate their understanding of literary elements (the curriculum), but they would maintain significant flexibility as they worked.

During my second year of teaching in Finland, my principal and I tried something new in history class. (It's common in Finland for principals to have a couple hours of teaching each week, by the way.) We invited the students— then sixth graders—to generate "juicy questions" in light of our current Finnish history unit. For inspiration, we encouraged them to flip through their readings and their notes. My students knew, from a previous study, that a juicy question differs from any old question, because it's a query that requires solid research and sound reasoning. Typically, it begins with *why* or *how*. Once students had developed a list of juicy questions—such as, why did it take so long for bronze to arrive in Finland?—my principal and I gave them the green light to circulate around the classroom and share their questions with one another. Their task was to find classmates who shared an interest in investigating a particular juicy question.

As these small groups formed, my principal and I met with each group to look at its juicy question, just to see if any tweaking was needed. Once small groups received our approval, they began researching their questions for the purpose of creating a large concept map with their findings.

Later, they presented these posters. This history project wasn't fancy, but I think it represented a decent connection between student interests and the curriculum, and our students seemed to enjoy it.

Providing our students with interesting curricular activities (as suggested by the Finnish early childhood educators) or open-ended assignments with built-in choices (like the Finnish history project) is a good step for promoting student autonomy in the classroom. But those strategies—in my opinion—don't compare with one simple, powerful gesture: planning with students.

Plan with your students

During my last month of teaching in Helsinki, I involved my students in planning more than I had ever done before, and in this area I chart my progress all the way back to my first week of teaching in Finland. If you recall from previous chapters, there was this one fifth grader, with angry red dots on his forehead, who nudged me to implement Finnish-style breaks, and then there was the feedback from my students about how they usually move around in the hallways, which saved me from the embarrassment of practicing with them how to walk in a straight line. From the beginning I had witnessed the power of involving my students in the planning process. My students had a lot of wisdom to offer, as long as I was willing to give them a voice in the classroom.

Before that first week of school in Finland, I had largely believed that planning was the sole responsibility of the teacher, and for years I missed out on a joyful practice, which effectively develops the agency of children. Since that first week of school, I have had several key experiences that reinforced the importance of planning with students. One of them occurred during an ethics unit, in which my small group of ten students and I studied the concept of democracy (then a central part of the fifth and sixth grade curriculum).

In a cluster of desks in the middle of our classroom, we discussed democracy at the macrolevel and identified its key ingredients. We also investigated the Finnish system of government, with the help of a Helsinki candidate running for a parliamentary position. However, the biggest highlight— from my perspective, at least—was a discussion about what democracy would look like in school.

To kick-start our lesson, I showed the students a You-Tube clip of the Sudbury Valley School, where students are given almost complete freedom in their learning. This model has been widely hailed as the embodiment of a truly democratic education, so I was curious to hear my sixth graders' reactions. I suspected that my students would fall in love with this unique approach, where so much freedom is granted to children.

At Sudbury Valley, students decide their own curriculum and structure their own days. Rules exist at the school, but they are enforced not by grownups but by a student-run disciplinary committee. A few adults are on standby throughout the school day, offering assistance when requested by the students. In this particular video clip, one teenage student confessed that, initially, he played computer games throughout each school day, but he eventually grew out of that phase.

In the conversation afterward, I was surprised to hear that many of my sixth graders felt that this model was too radical. Specifically, a couple of my students seemed upset that some Sudbury Valley students were wasting school days on computer games. Their criticism shocked me a little, because the most outspoken children in my classroom were the ones who seemed to spend a significant amount of their free time on digital devices. That day, my sixth grade ethics class was suggesting to me that they *didn't* want to do schooling alone. They wanted autonomy, of course, but they also didn't want the Sudbury Valley model of (nearly) total freedom. This distinction has stuck with me.

That general reaction of my ethics students brought me unexpected relief because, before this discussion, I thought that, once they had heard about a model like Sudbury Valley School, they'd express resentment about the more traditional teacher–student arrangement at my school and so many others. Instead, my students seemed to want a *combination* of teacher leadership and student leadership.

This is where the notion of coplanning—sharing the responsibility of determining the direction of learning—makes so much sense. It allows teachers and students to work together to make the most out of school. As Finland seeks to emphasize the importance of developing student agency in its new curriculum reform, it's requiring that all Finnish comprehensive schools (grade one to grade nine) develop and offer one interdisciplinary unit of study, which is of particular interest to the children, per school year for all students. Additionally, it's expected that the children help to plan these interdisciplinary units of study (Halinen, 2015).

As I was becoming more of a believer in planning *with* my students, I decided to cocreate an ethics project with my sixth graders after our study of democracy. We turned to another concept in our curriculum: sustainable development. After defining it in basic terms, my students and I started to design a final unit together. (That felt right, after investigating this idea of a democratic school.)

We brainstormed different examples of sustainable development, and one of the topics that seemed to interest my sixth graders was clean energy—specifically, the use of solar energy. Many of my students heard about a project at our school, involving older classmates, in which they planned to install solar panels. Given my sixth graders' enthusiasm, we decided to investigate this particular area of sustainable development as our final unit. I wish there had been more time in the school year, because my students were buzzing with ideas as we designed our study. Originally, we talked about the idea of purchasing solar panels for classroom use. (One of my sixth graders, I remember, even provided me with a price quote he had found online.)

In the end, we decided to do something quite modest. My class would invite the teacher who was overseeing the school's solar energy initiative to a presentation in our classroom. My students would share their learning about solar panels with this teacher, with the intent of teaching this "expert" something new. We also allocated time to hear more about our school's project from my colleague. And as something fun, my students planned to design a Kahoot! quiz (based on the content of their presentation) as a way to better engage their audience, which would include several younger students accompanied by my colleague.

Because it was the very end of the school year, I remember that we only had a couple of weeks (only about four classroom hours) to prepare. But my ethics students, in that short period of time, continued to prove to me the instructional value of coplanning. During the preparation phase, I saw their level of motivation increase, along with their level of interest and their commitment to high-quality work. Presenting on solar panels wasn't a graded project, but I saw my small group of ten sixth graders working harder than I had ever seen them work on graded group work.

The first thing we did as a class—after we decided on the basic components of that day—was briefly design an outline for the slideshow (based on my students' questions about solar panels). Once we had this basic framework, my sixth graders started to research their questions in small groups, using their smartphones. Our class computer was used primarily to prepare the slideshow, an effort led by a couple of students. As they started the first draft of the presentation, they displayed it on the screen at the front of our classroom, so that everyone in the classroom could see their progress. I remember a couple of my students, without my recommendation or direction, uploaded their slideshow presentation to Google Drive and began sharing it with one another, as a way to collaborate outside of school. It wasn't homework, but they saw their presentation as important enough to make it their homework. As you'd expect, I felt pretty happy.

When the day of the presentation rolled around, my students were ready. As they took turns sharing their learning in front of my colleague and her class, their ownership was clear. They spoke articulately and passionately about solar energy. And when my colleague told my students more about our school's project, it felt like a refreshing exchange of learning. The icing on the cake was the fun, student-designed Kahoot! quiz after the presentation.

There are so many ways to do coplanning. What matters most is that teachers carve out time *before* launching a unit or a project, to discuss the direction of the learning with their students, and then draw upon that discussion to shape the unit or project.

Throughout my teaching career, I've sometimes wielded a popular instructional strategy called a KWL chart, developed by Donna Ogle in the 1980s, to kick off units of study, but I admit that I've often treated this exercise more as an obligation than something that has the potential to significantly impact learning during the unit. A teacher uses a KWL chart to write down (typically on a piece of chart paper or poster board divided into three columns) what students *know* already about a particular curriculum-related subject, what they *want* to know about it, and then, once the unit kicks off, what students have *learned* about that topic. (The KWL strategy can be used with stand-alone lessons, too.) Here's an example of how a KWL chart can appear:

Things I *know* about: _____

Things I *want* to know about: _____

Things I *learned* about: _____

A KWL chart is a sensible way of building background knowledge and helping students see how they've grown in their knowledge, but the problem I've had with KWL charts lies in the middle column. Often my students would share earnestly what they want to know about a particular curriculum-related subject, such as water or the life cycle of an animal, but ultimately these specific areas of interest recorded on the KWL chart are not used to impact the direction of the unit in any meaningful way. Perhaps the middle column is useful because it gets kids excited to learn something new, but I think students benefit from having more ownership in the planning process. As teachers who want to coplan, we need to put more of an emphasis on the question, what do you want to know?

Years ago I attended a week-long institute on the subject of differentiated instruction, led by Carol Ann Tomlinson at the University of Virginia, and I'll never forget what happened before it started. The evening before the kickoff, all of the participants gathered in an auditorium, and we were divided into small groups, facilitated by the university's graduate students. Those facilitators invited us to share our interests regarding differentiated instruction, and they furiously wrote them down on pieces of chart paper in different corners of the auditorium.

As I was returning to my hotel, I spotted Tomlinson outside of the auditorium clutching those rolled-up sheets of chart paper, and I imagined that she was on her way home, where she would spread out those pieces of paper on her kitchen table and study our feedback that same evening. Despite having taught this institute numerous times before, Tomlinson signaled that she wanted to let us, the "students," shape the learning of that entire week. That's *coplanning*, where students are given a voice, and then their feedback is used to impact the direction of learning.

Make it real

It's 9:45 A.M., and the "game" officially begins in one hour. Dozens of Finnish sixth-graders are standing nervously in cubicles in a 6,000 square-foot space resembling a miniature city, equipped with its own city hall, grocery store, and bank.

Many of the children are whispering and finger-pointing, as they adjust to this unusual learning environment during their brief orientation. Each student has been assigned a profession (such as a reporter, a sales associate, or a custodian) in a particular business, in a specific cubicle, where he or she will work until the last shift ends at 1:25 P.M.

For weeks, these sixth-graders have prepared in their classrooms for this one-day visit, studying the topics of entrepreneurship, working life, citizenship, and the economy. In their cubicles, these 12- and 13-year-olds carefully review their daily schedules and professional responsibilities on tablet computers, as trained adults offer their assistance. Meanwhile, their classroom teachers are encouraged to sit back and relax; some of them elect to sip coffee from the city's tiny cafe as they watch the action unfold.

The first shift begins at 10:45 A.M., and the miniature city springs to life. The profit of every business is at stake, as is its reputation. Some children start with free time, in which they fetch their own bank cards, allowing them to purchase goods and services from the city's other businesses. Most sixth-graders begin working: Bosses pay the salaries of employees (through a digital banking system) and establish contracts with the city's energy and waste-management companies, while other professionals turn their attention to customer service. The place buzzes as the 80 children role-play.

This school year, more than 70 percent of Finland's sixth-graders have undertaken a similar experience through a program called *Yrityskylä* ("Me & MyCity" in English). This initiative has gained traction in this Nordic country, growing from a 2010 pilot group of 800 sixth-graders to 45,000 students annually, who visit one of eight different locations. The Me & MyCity program is organized by Finland's Economic Information Office (a 70-year-old nonprofit), and its costs are covered through the Ministry of Education and Culture, municipalities, private foundations, and a handful of Finnish corporations that are featured as actual businesses in the learning environment (Walker, 2016d).

Although Me & MyCity is already internationally recognized as innovative, this Finnish learning model was in part inspired by an American program called "BizTown," started by an organization called Junior Achievement. According to Pasi Sahlberg, Finland has a habit of borrowing pedagogical ideas from the United States, developing them, and implementing them on a national scale (Walker, 2016d). But why hasn't America done the same with its own innovative learning concepts?

Sahlberg told me it has to do with a difference in national educational policy: "Much of what goes on in American schools is about what school boards decide," he said in an email. But in Finland, Sahlberg explained, there is a clear, agreed-upon national educational policy, which "sets the priorities, values, and main directions for the entire system"— and this ultimately provides the nation's educators with sufficient leeway to implement ideas like Me & MyCity.

The learning benefits of Me & MyCity are compelling, based on research presented at the Association of European Economics Education conference in August, 2016. In this recent study, about 900 Finnish sixth-graders completed two surveys (a pre- and post-test) with multiple-choice questions seeking to gauge their economic knowledge and (reported) savings behavior. Here's a sample question: "A library is a public service. How are its costs covered?" Based on the results, Panu Kalmi—a professor of economics at Finland's University of Vaasa and the author of the study—concluded that participation in Me & MyCity was "clearly" associated with greater economic knowledge. Furthermore, more than 75 percent of sixth-graders reported that the program increased their interest in economic issues and saving money. According to Kalmi, this shows that these students felt motivated by Me & MyCity. In fact, the researcher found that those sixth-graders whose interest in saving money had grown substantially (after completing the program) also reported a significant increase in their own savings behavior (Walker, 2016d).

"My students were extremely motivated [by Me & MyCity]," Mona Paalanen, a Finnish elementary-school teacher who taught sixth-graders in Helsinki last year, said in an email. Many of Paalanen's sixth-graders had already heard about Me & MyCity before she announced their participation in the program, and "for once" she didn't need to motivate her kids to do their schoolwork, given their soaring enthusiasm. One of the most exciting moments for Paalanen and her class was a round of job interviews she conducted prior to their one-day visit, which was something the program's curriculum encouraged. One by one, she met with her students, grilling them with questions about the roles they wanted to play in the miniature city. After the interviews, her sixth-graders laughed about how "tough" she had been, and how it had been "a bit scary." That same day, one parent emailed her asking if her daughter could have an interview over the phone, since her child was too sick to come into school. Her sixth-grader badly wanted to interview for the job of mayor. Paalanen told me that her student's "devotion" helped her to win this job.

In conversations with other Finnish teachers who have experienced Me & MyCity, I've heard a common takeaway: The program was exceptionally motivating for students, and this appeared to boost the learning, both in the classroom-setting and in the 6,000 square-foot learning space. When my Helsinki students participated in the program, I had the same impression.

On the big day, my sixth graders were nervously excited. I watched from the sidelines as they worked like little adults in their different professions. Admittedly, I felt proud seeing them do their jobs competently, and most of them possessed a glow of satisfaction throughout the one-day experience. However, it wasn't a smooth ride for everyone.

In at least one group, there was a breakdown in collaboration among workers. And although this issue wasn't easily resolved during the day, it was a realistic problem in any job setting. It was *exactly* the kind of learning all students would benefit from having as they head into the working world one day.

All in all, Me & MyCity was a special experience for my class. And it looked like a celebration *and* an application of their learning. When classroom learning resembles real-world learning, it's easier for kids to see the intended purpose of their schoolwork.

As a teacher, I see my professional learning as directly connected to my vocation. When I learn how to teach better, I experience joy. I know I'm not the only one because I've met many educators—in America, Finland, and elsewhere—who are also driven by this sense of professional purpose.

But I've often detected a disconnect in schools. Just because teachers may feel a strong sense of purpose in the classroom, their students may not. Children, I've found, usually need our help seeing how their schoolwork connects to the "real world."

Throughout my teaching career I've known this to be true, and yet, while I've tried a few small things to make learning more purposeful for my students, I admit that I've often felt lost. (Confession: I haven't always grasped the classroom–to–real-world connection myself.)

I used to think it was enough to *tell* my students the rationale for learning something (a math concept, for example). But my words rarely seemed to satisfy their need to understand their work's relevance. As is so often the case, I've needed good models to show me how to make learning more real for kids. I'm grateful to have witnessed a few strong examples in Finnish classrooms, in addition to seeing the Me & MyCity program in action.

Once, I walked into Paula Havu's first grade classroom at my Helsinki school, and I found tiny children with real needles in their hands. It was especially scary, because I couldn't find Paula initially. (Eventually I saw her sitting at a little table coaching a child in how to sew.) I was impressed that my colleague's students were using real needles, but she seemed a little dissatisfied with the lesson. Paula confided that her only regret was that the needles weren't sharp enough.

In my colleague's classroom in Helsinki, I didn't see little blond boys sword fighting with the needles; they were using them for their intended purpose: learning how to sew. Using real needles in the classroom might feel a little too risky for many of us teachers (myself included), but Paula was clearly making the schoolwork more relevant for her students by creating a more realistic context for learning.

I saw a similar phenomenon in the woodworking classroom, which looked much more like a carpenter's workshop (the size of three or four traditional classrooms). One afternoon I delivered a message to my colleague, the woodworking teacher, and out of curiosity I circulated around the classroom to see how my students were progressing in their work. In one corner of the classroom I found one of my students welding. He was wearing a protective mask with a large visor, and in one hand, he held a blowtorch!

Two floors above the woodworking classroom was the home economics classroom, another strange learning environment, with kitchenettes, large knives, a refrigerator, and a washing machine to clean dirty aprons. During my two years of teaching in Helsinki, I'd make several visits to this classroom, and each time I found students deeply engaged in their work. I think the level of freedom allowed by the home economics teacher had something to do with it (the kids would prepare everything themselves), but I believe there were other factors, too.

One major factor, I'd argue, was the clear purpose of their work. These teens were learning how to cook, which was something they'd take with them into adulthood. And that overarching purpose brought greater significance to the (relatively) mundane aspects of the students' learning, such as cleaning dishes, setting the table, and managing the laundry.

In one Finnish kindergarten classroom, I had seen children running an ice cream shop, with fake ice cream and fake money. Indeed, the arrangement could have been more real if the teachers had offered their students actual cash and actual ice cream, but I think this fairly low-prep gesture did a solid job of connecting the math learning to the real world. (For the record, a kindergarten teacher at this Finnish preschool told me that they would occasionally take their students to a nearby ice cream kiosk and buy frozen treats with real money provided by the parents.)

Wielding the strategy *make it real* doesn't need to look as ambitious as Me & MyCity, or even as significant as setting up an ice cream station in your classroom—it can look as tiny as the decision to use real needles. The goal of *make it real* is to promote a sense of purpose in the classroom, which will ultimately bring joy to learners.

Demand responsibility

Through teaching in Helsinki and interviewing Finnish teachers, I kept hearing the word "responsibility" repeated. I wasn't used to hearing this word in conversations with American educators. Instead, the substitute word I heard most often in the United States was accountability. Although educators in Finland aren't held accountable by standardized tests or school inspections, I'd argue that this low level of accountability works in Finnish schools because there's a high level of professional responsibility, which is afforded by a high level of professional trust.

The idea that Finland's teachers are trusted more than America's teachers is one that I've heard repeated in education circles, and I've heard different theories for why Finland's teachers garner this level of societal confidence. One popular theory is that the status of teachers is sky-high in Finland. To become qualified, Finns must complete the equivalent of a master's degree in the field of education. Unlike America, Finland has only a handful of university teaching programs, where the acceptance rate is famously low, and education students are required to complete a rigorous master's thesis. Teach for America, the organization that's famous for recruiting high-achieving U.S. college graduates and depositing them in urban American schools, is known for requiring five weeks of training. Finland's elementary education program requires five years.

While I do think that Finland's teachers are generally trusted more than America's teachers, I think it's less about a difference in status and more about a difference in culture. In both countries, I've met many hardworking, dependable educators. I think the problem in America's school system, in this regard, is that there's too much emphasis on "accountability," which is fear based, and too little emphasis on "responsibility," which is trust based.

Beginning at an early age, Finnish children are trusted with many responsibilities. If you remember, the vast majority of my Helsinki students were commuting to and from school on a daily basis. I noticed subtle things, too, such as little kids—the age of kindergartners—roaming around Helsinki's parks without parents, or children serving themselves food in the school cafeteria, or kids walking the hallways without their teachers. These children weren't trusted with these responsibilities because they were "high status" individuals; they were trusted because adults believed they could be successful on their own.

Educators in Finland experience something similar, in my opinion. I've found that Finland's administrators and parents trust the nation's teachers because they respect their professionalism. I've detected a common belief that teachers can do their jobs well, without external pressure—and, in the end, everyone seems happier that way. Fear-driven accountability efforts can essentially squeeze out opportunities for a person to experience the joy of exercising meaningful responsibility.

This applies to both adults and children. Recently, I've seen this dynamic play out in my relationship with my son, Misaiel. When Misaiel was four years old, he figured out how to lower and raise the windows in the car. Initially my wife and I were a little worried about his newfound skill. Although he was securely strapped into his car seat, lacking the ability to get out on his own, we *feared* that he would (somehow) fall out of the car. So, we'd exert accountability by letting him lower the window only by a few inches, and then we'd lock his window.

But our lack of trust, evidenced by his locked window, greatly bothered our four-year-old. Suddenly, the activity of lowering his window no longer seemed satisfying to him, and he'd often pout on those car rides. After a few experiences like this one, we told our son that we'd try something new—we'd no longer lock the window, to see if he could be successful on his own. Once my wife and I made this change, we saw his attitude shift immediately for the better, and he continued to respect our rule of only a few inches.

Initially, due to our fear and our lack of trust, we had provided him so little freedom that he lacked meaningful responsibility. But when we showed him that we would trust him to carry out his responsibility to manage the window, he was successful *and* happy.

While it's infeasible to think that the American school system could import Finland's culture of trust, we teachers can bring this same attitude into our classrooms by trusting our students with a little more autonomy, in order to give them more opportunities to assume age-appropriate responsibilities. Earlier in this chapter, I suggested the strategy *start with freedom*, which is certainly an approach that requires trust, but the strategy I'm suggesting in this section, *demand responsibility*, goes one step further. It's more like a guiding principle that teachers can seek to apply every day in their classrooms, not just at the beginning of a lesson or a unit.

Taru Pohtola, a foreign language teacher in the Finnish city of Vantaa and a 2015–2016 Fulbright scholar who was based in Indiana for the fall semester, told me that she believes that giving students more responsibility in the classroom will also reduce the stress that American teachers experience:

> I can't generalize, but I noticed that it was quite common in many American schools (at least a lot more common than in Finland) for teachers, for example, to collect their students' homework every single day and spend hours grading these assignments, every single day. The teachers might feel the need to do so because of the pressure of standardized tests, and so on, but it might be quite stressful for students, too, if everything is constantly evaluated. I wondered whether it might also reduce the actual joy of learning. In Finland, even though we do give homework and the students do various things in class and at home, we hardly ever grade their homework (only some specific

assignments). What we do is go over the work and exercises with the students in class together. Everything is considered part of the learning process. Giving the students more responsibility is naturally one way to reduce the workload of teachers, but taking responsibility is also an important skill the students need in life, and I believe it's important to let them practice it.

As teachers, we can provide our students with responsibilities in the area of assessment, too. Taru told me she has learned to let her students evaluate themselves more and sometimes allows them to grade their own papers. According to her, it has reduced her workload and stress:

> For example, instead of me correcting small vocabulary tests and grading them myself, I can just show the students the correct answers right away and let them check how well they did. This way I might be able to focus on something more important perhaps than testing, and I believe the students also eventually learn more this way since they get immediate feedback. Even a "test" can be considered a learning event. I can still collect these "tests" at the end to see who needs more help and practice, for example. I get the same information as I would have gotten if I had corrected everything myself, but I have saved a lot of time.

There are many ways we can encourage responsibility taking in our classrooms, but no matter what we decide to do, it starts with trust. Will we allow our students, on a regular basis, enough freedom to take meaningful responsibility of their learning? There's risk involved in providing reasonable freedoms to the children in our classroom (they might fail!), but the potential benefits are outstanding: less stress, a lighter workload for teachers, and, best of all, more student ownership of learning, which facilitates their academic success and their joy.

When I started teaching in Finland, I panicked a little when I noticed that there weren't enough binders, or folders, for all of my fifth graders. Along with other classroom teachers at my Helsinki school, I had been provided with new notebooks: lined, gridded, and blank ones. How, I wondered, were my students going to keep track of all the loose-leaf sheets of paper without binders or folders? In the United States, I don't think I ever saw a student survive on *just* notebooks.

Thankfully, I found enough (cardboard) magazine holders for my Helsinki fifth graders to use, and I distributed them to my students for organizational purposes. They kept them on their desks, and my students would usually throw their loose-leaf sheets into them. Over time, I detected a major problem: my system of organization and the handouts I gave them weren't exactly helping them to stay organized. Often I'd provide them with graphic organizers, and then I'd see these sheets pile up in their cardboard containers. Eventually their magazine holders started to overflow, and after school I'd sometimes find their handouts or books scattered around the classroom—then I'd deliver their misplaced work into their storage spaces. Also, I noticed that, although I had given them notebooks, I wasn't giving them enough opportunities to take notes, so I'd find a lack of organization *inside* of their notebooks.

After that first year ended, I threw away all of those cardboard magazine holders (most of them were in pretty bad shape already), and I decided that I'd try something different the following year. I'd do what I saw many of my Helsinki colleagues doing with their students: provide my students with only notebooks. The children would take responsibility for keeping track of their things.

This was a simple shift, but that next year I saw my students improve in the area of organization. Rarely did I find their work lying around the classroom after school. That year I decided it would be better for me to go easy on the graphic organizers, so that my students could take care of this responsibility of jotting down information, and I saw their note-taking skills improve, too.

Through this experience, I learned that limiting "crutches," such as magazine holders and graphic organizers, ultimately helped my students develop their own methods for staying organized. It had become clearer to me: I had an important role as a teacher to cultivate a classroom where students had enough freedom to take responsibility over their own learning.

Mastery

ON DECEMBER 4, 2001, THE FIRST PISA RESULTS were published, and among the member nations of the Organization of Economic Cooperation and Development, Finland was the highest performing in all three academic areas: reading, mathematics, and science (Sahlberg, 2015). In *Finnish Lessons 2.0* (2015), Pasi Sahlberg offers this analysis:

> This new international study revealed that earlier student performance gaps with Japan, Korea, and Hong Kong were closed. Finns seemed to learn all the knowledge and skills they demonstrated on these tests without private tutoring, after-school classes, or the large amounts of

homework that are particularly prevalent among students in East Asia. Furthermore, the relative variation of educational performance between schools in the sample was exceptionally small in Finland. . . . The next two PISA cycles, in 2003 and 2006, advanced and consolidated Finland's reputation even further, thus elevating the world media's interest in Finnish education. (Chapter 1, loc. 1215–1228)

Although the academic results of Finland's fifteen-year-olds dipped in the 2009, 2012, and 2015 PISA cycles, the PISA data broadly reveal that this Nordic nation, according to Sahlberg, "[produces] consistently high learning results regardless of their students' socioeconomic status" (Chapter 1, loc. 1232).

To be happy, one of the basic things that we must have is feeling competent in a particular area, such as sculpting, coding, or writing. Raj Raghunathan (2016) says it is our demand for mastery. As teachers, we can infuse our classrooms with joy by addressing this need for expertise. Through teaching in Helsinki and visiting schools throughout Finland, I've gathered a handful of classroom strategies for developing mastery, inspired by Finnish educators: *teach the essentials, leverage the tech, coach more, prove the learning,* and *discuss the grades.*

Teach the essentials

While I taught in the United States, I found myself gravitating toward inspiring models of teaching, such as differentiated instruction, Responsive Classroom, and project-based learning (PBL). As a teacher, each of these approaches offered me something useful. Differentiated instruction encouraged me to consider the needs of all of my learners and then how to teach flexibly in order to address them. Responsive Class-room provided me with a framework for social-emotional learning, which served as the foundation of my classroom. And PBL gave me a holistic approach for organizing the curriculum. I considered each of these methodologies to be exciting and challenging. That being said, the most demand-ing model to implement, in my opinion, was PBL.

Different definitions of PBL exist, but I'll explain how I have come to understand this interdisciplinary approach to teaching. A PBL unit is typically organized around the com-pletion of an authentic, high-quality product, which a teacher and students find interesting and motivating. In my experi-ence, the product (which may be a class book, a student-directed play, an app, and so on) is the most important aspect of the unit, because it's designed to represent and drive the interdisciplinary learning.

Typically, PBL units are led by science or social studies content, with reading and writing goals always integrated. In PBL, the idea is to make the curriculum come to life, where students experience interdisciplinary learning, ser-vice, fieldwork, and visits from experts as they seek to make a meaningful, high-quality product.

When I started teaching in Finland, I was eager to bring PBL into my Helsinki classroom. Equipped with my school's five-hundred-page curriculum document, I started to plan—beginning in July—a big interdisciplinary unit, even before I had met my principal and seen my teaching schedule. My idea was that we'd begin the year with a bang. Unfortu-nately, I think the opposite occurred.

In my planning, I titled the PBL unit Pathways to the Olympics, and my idea was that we'd use the Olympics as an interesting lens for my students to learn the required history and geography content. In this ten-week unit, I imagined that we'd "walk through the centuries" by first investigating the Olympics in a study of ancient Greece, and then we'd gradually progress to modern history. Once I had this organizing principle in mind, I recorded which objectives and content areas we'd specifically address in this PBL unit, based on my school's curriculum.

To breathe life into this unit, I invited a Finnish Olympian and her coach into our classroom. Additionally, before the school year began, I contacted a Finnish Paralympian, who graciously agreed to work with my students on a possible service project, in which my class would help raise money for underfunded, young Finnish Paralympians.

Here's a lightly edited description I wrote in my unit plan, during the summer of 2013 (days before I started my teaching stint in Helsinki):

> Pathways to the Olympics is specifically designed to develop respect, student ownership of learning, empathy, the inquiry–learning cycle, and a culture of high quality in the classroom while learning essential understandings, knowledge, and skills in geography, history, and English language arts. Additionally, the students will participate in meaningful service that will benefit young Paralympians. Fieldwork and visits from experts will enrich the process of learning.
>
> In project based learning, one or two content areas will often take the lead; in this case, it's geography and history. Literacy skills will always be integrated. What does this mean for science content this

year? It means that science content will lead during the next project. The bottom line is that all of the content of this year will be engaged by the students. More than one or two content areas may overlap at times, but not always. This is done for the sake of achieving deeper learning in each subject.

Students will be knee-deep in writing during this ten-week study. Keeping a student blog will be something that's required of every student. For the first three weeks, we will be doing our blog posts in school, which means that we will be emphasizing high-quality work. Additionally, we will be doing other homework assignments (in reading and math) at school during the first weeks, too.

Although there are many skills that need to be learned in the beginning of the year, there is a sense of urgency about learning history content. Creating a class wiki would capture our learning along the way and encourage the degree in which we engage the content. Since we will be investigating thousands of years of history, we need ways to track our walk through the centuries.

Can you detect the problem(s) in my plan? There are several I've found, but the major one, in my opinion, was the significant number of demanding, novel initiatives: student blogging, a class wiki, a major fundraising campaign for Paralympians. I see nothing inherently wrong with any of these ingredients, but the plan didn't seem like it was rooted in the essentials of the curriculum, nor, as I mentioned earlier, was it based on my students' interests, necessarily.

As I reread my project description, it appears as if I was trying to make the curriculum serve the activities, not the other way around. I had fallen in love with my idea of making everything connected to the Olympics. When a teacher writes "since we will be investigating thousands of years of history" you know that plan is in *deep* trouble. In my effort to implement PBL in Finland, I ultimately failed because I didn't have a good handle on the contents of my school's curriculum.

I think there were several reasons that my PBL unit Pathways to the Olympics never got off the ground. One major problem was that my plan lacked focus: I didn't let the curricular objectives and content lead the unit. My early flop in Helsinki revealed a weakness in my teaching: I could get distracted by the auxiliary aspects of planning classroom instruction. During those early weeks of school, for example, I spent a significant amount of time arranging inspirational visits from Olympians and Paralympians, launching student blogging, and fretting about fundraising for a young Paralympic team. Those *weren't* essential tasks.

With an American teaching schedule in the Boston area, where I had significantly more instructional time each week, this problem of getting distracted in my planning was never apparent to me. I could afford to keep my units and lessons a little loose around the edges. Sure, I'd always *aim* to teach the essentials, but I think often I didn't plan as efficiently as I could have.

In Finland, where I had much less time with my students, there just wasn't time to maintain loose connections to content and objectives in my classroom. I needed to prepare tighter units and tighter lessons. It wasn't my ideal way of planning, but the limited hours of instruction demanded it. That new environment pushed me to put the auxiliary aspects of planning where they belong—in a supporting role. That first year of teaching in Helsinki, I had certain subjects with my fifth graders where we'd meet only once each week for forty-five minutes: biology and geography, chemistry and physics, and ethics. Also, I felt squeezed in math, because we had only *three* forty-five-minute periods. Honestly, I felt pinched for time in every subject I taught.

When I first started teaching in Finland, I found this lighter schedule to be a blessing and a curse. It was wonderful to have *more* time to plan and collaborate with colleagues, but it was also a curse to have *less* time to teach my students. In Helsinki, my Finnish colleagues helped me to conceive of planning in a different way, to focus on teaching the essentials. Given that lessons in several subjects were in short supply, I found that my fellow teachers were adept at budgeting lessons. In my experience planning with them, I'd sometimes hear them talk about the number of remaining lessons in a term, and then plan backward, with the curriculum and materials close at hand.

Through observing Finnish classrooms, I've found that Finland's most popular methods of promoting mastery in the classroom aren't exactly cutting edge. Contrary to what I initially expected, Finland's teachers typically employ traditional, teacher-directed classroom instruction.

As one of my Finnish colleagues informed me during my first year of teaching in Helsinki, textbooks are a tradition in Finland's schools. Even Finland's first graders, typically, spend a significant amount of classroom time completing exercises from workbooks in different subjects. In my dozens of hours of observing classrooms throughout Finland, I'd often see textbooks, lecturing, and students copying text off the blackboard (or whiteboard) into their notebooks. This "on the ground" picture of classroom instruction in Finland didn't match the glowing image represented by the international media—and, initially, I didn't know what to make of this finding.

One of the reasons that Finnish teachers seem to embrace textbooks, I've deduced, is that those materials help them to pace their units and their lessons. It's common, I've found, for the chapters of Finnish textbooks to correspond with the number of lessons in a particular subject. For example, if there are thirty-six lessons of history in a school year, it's reasonable to expect to find thirty-six chapters in that subject's textbook.

This notion that Finland's teachers keep their classroom instruction fairly rigid may seem paradoxical, given the reputation that they have for having so much freedom in their work. But I think it's this characteristic that gives them stability in their day-to-day efforts, allowing them and their students to master content areas.

For years, I've been seeking to improve as a teacher, but I admit that it's only recently that I've felt much more focused in my instructional planning. With this strategy, *teach the essentials*, I'm not suggesting that teachers abandon student-centered practices for teacher-directed practices. Instead, I'm recommending that we adopt a healthy sense of urgency in our planning, in an effort to prioritize the essentials, based on the curricula.

In Finland, once I started reallocating my planning time by aligning my lesson plans and units more closely with the curriculum, I found that it was easier for my students to achieve mastery in our classroom. They *needed* me to prioritize the essentials in our classroom and not get distracted by auxiliary aspects of teaching, such as inviting Olympians and launching student blogging. One of the best ways to stay focused, I've found, is through a practice I call *mine the textbook.*

Mine the textbook

While teaching in the United States, I was a little suspicious of commercial curricula. Subtly, these materials were marketed as "teacher-proof," an idea that any literate person could follow the scripted lessons found in the teaching guides. Among my fellow American teachers I detected resentment, because sticking to the curriculum ("following the script") limited their creativity and ultimately diminished their sense of professionalism. I remember meeting one new teacher in an American public school who seemed horrified by the pressure to keep pace with her math curriculum, one scripted lesson per day; she knew that many of her kids weren't learning the math content, but she felt pressure to plow ahead anyway.

Some American educators I've known mistrust the commercial curricula because they question the motives of the publishing companies. They wonder, are these learning materials designed with children's best interests in mind? I've heard the argument that commercial curricula can sometimes serve as a tool to prepare students for standardized tests, which are designed by the same publishing company.

But in Finland, I discovered, my Finnish colleagues appeared to possess a much more positive view of commercial curricula. It surprised me—instead of dreading the stuff, they appeared to embrace the materials. In the fall of my first year in Helsinki, one of my Finnish colleagues, then a first-year teacher, praised the commercial curricula she used. As we chatted in her classroom, she held up different teaching guides, assuring me that these materials were designed by actual classroom practitioners. In other words, this teacher trusted the curricula. Her view of the textbooks was pragmatic. She reasoned, if these resources are solid, why would I *not* use them in my classroom?

I understood my colleague's point, but I couldn't help but notice how this teacher's embrace of the commercial curricula contrasted sharply with what I would often observe in American schools. My Helsinki colleagues signaled that they viewed the use of these materials as valuable in their classrooms, not as a joy-diminishing obligation. According to teachers I spoke with, the curricula helped them teach well; specifically, the resources helped them to stay focused on essential content, keep pace, and lighten the planning load, so they wouldn't have to prepare units and lessons from scratch.

In Finland my attitude toward commercial curricula changed significantly. I started to see these materials as very useful resources. I wasn't going to let "the textbook" be the master of my classroom and follow it to a tee, but I *was* going to do something I hadn't done much of in America: mine the textbook.

In his book *The Well-Balanced Teacher* (2010), Mike Anderson, a veteran educator and teaching consultant, describes a similar shift in his approach to textbooks:

After a few years, I started to move away from using the math curriculum as my sole teaching tool and began to think of it more as a resource. I followed the general scope and sequence of the math book, using the activities that fit my students particularly well. Some games in the program were especially fun and useful. I then created my own lessons that fit the goals and guidelines of the curriculum that were more engaging—more hands-on with more differentiation and choice for students—and skipped lessons that were particularly bland or developmentally a bad fit for my students. We created a geometric quilt using the framework of the chapter on geometry that we proudly hung in our classroom. We did scavenger hunts around the classroom and the school for real-world uses of fractions and decimals. We played games to practice place value. Not only did the students enjoy math more, but so did I! The daily lessons were more fun for me because I knew that they matched my students' needs and that students would enjoy them. The planning itself was fun as I became deeply engaged in the creative process of crafting lessons and activities based on what was best for my students. Instead of feeling like the robotic conduit of the scripted math curriculum, I felt like a teacher again. (pp. 85–86)

Over those two years in Helsinki, I found that the approach of many of my Finnish colleagues was wise: solid commercial learning materials, when used strategically, help kids master content. Ideally, the curricular resources that are given to you as a teacher are high-quality. But even when they're not, I've found that they're still usable.

"Keep the good stuff," says Anderson, "and make it the focus" (p. 86). In Helsinki, my principal and I taught sixth grade history together, and we'd often flip through the students' textbook, using only the content relevant for our class. The kids needed an anchor text, and the textbook, although flawed, served this purpose. My principal and I weren't plodding through the history textbook—we were mining it.

As I taught math in Helsinki, I often followed the commercial curriculum (I thought it was well sequenced), but I encouraged my students to take a critical perspective as they completed practice problems. Their math textbooks were translated from Finnish into English, and on many occasions they identified subtle errors made by the publishing company. In their ongoing attempt to outsmart these materials, they worked hard to understand the math.

In recent history, the country of Estonia has performed well on the PISA, especially in math. So when a group of Estonian educators visited my Helsinki school, I was eager to talk to them about their nation's success on these international tests. Over lunch I chatted with one Estonian teacher, and when I mentioned that I had observed a culture of textbook usage in Finland's classrooms, she told me that she had seen the same thing in Estonia. It was something she thought that helped explain her country's success on the PISA. I wondered, too, if Finland's consistently high performance on international tests could be partly attributed to teachers using commercial curricula skillfully in their classrooms.

As teachers, if we want to promote mastery, we don't need to, as one 2015 teaching book is assuredly titled, *Ditch That Textbook*. We can mine the textbook and use those learning materials in a way that supports good teaching and learning.

Leverage the tech

When I first visited my Helsinki school, my Finnish principal gave me a tour. She showed me my classroom, the teachers' lounge, and our library. She also wanted to show me the school's two computer labs, which were shared by my colleagues and about 450 students. At this urban public school in the middle of Helsinki, I think I had modest expectations about the technology I would discover.

Years ago, before I became a classroom teacher, I worked at a complex of four primary schools in a poor urban neighborhood in Massachusetts as a substitute computer teacher, and although the district seemed underfunded—one school even fired its only secretary while I was there—they possessed stunning Mac labs with about twenty-five new-looking desktop computers in each one. Every few years, these devices would be replaced. Annually, the complex would employ two full-time computer teachers and an information technology specialist, who would oversee all of the tech equipment and software. As I walked with my Finnish principal through my Helsinki school, which was located in a much wealthier neighborhood than those Massachusetts public schools, I expected to find something similar to what I had seen in America.

The first lab I visited at my Helsinki school held about twenty laptops, which looked as if they had been purchased about ten years earlier. Later, I noticed a section on the blackboard where teachers could write down which laptops— each one had a number—was out of service; several of them were completely broken. Although this lab didn't meet my expectations, I bit my tongue as we walked through that room and climbed two flights of stairs to another set of computers. That second lab, I thought, wasn't much different from the previous one. There were about twenty-five desktop computers, and to my eyes, all of them looked like they were soon due for replacement.

Typically every classroom in my school had one desktop computer, an adjacent "doc camera" and a projector that could display images on a pull-down screen. A few classrooms had SMART Boards, but there wasn't a discernible push from the administration for teachers to use them. Unlike my experience at those urban public schools in America, my school didn't employ a full-time computer teacher. Educators were expected to use the technology as they saw fit, and when problems would (inevitably) arise, we were directed to contact a couple of tech-savvy teachers who were modestly compensated for their help.

Technology integration, at my Helsinki school, wasn't a major emphasis, and this was something I observed at other Finnish schools. Before moving to Finland, I expected that all high-quality schools would have the best and the latest tech equipment. But I've changed my mind since spending time in Finnish schools, where the investment in technology seems to lag behind what I've seen in American schools.

In Helsinki, I found that it was easier to put learning first in the classroom setting when my access (and my students' access) to technology was limited. I didn't have the same pressure—internal or external—to integrate technology, which meant that I was more likely to use tech when it enhanced the teaching.

I don't believe classroom technologies are unimportant. Truly, there is a digital divide in our schools that must be addressed, but in many schools the investment of money and time seems too great. Those flashy technologies can easily distract us teachers from working on the most essential things with our students. I know this from personal experience, and research seems to suggest this, too.

In 2015, the Organization for Economic Cooperation and Development (OECD), the same organization that designed the PISA tests, published the results of a PISA assessment of digital skills. It found that, "overall, students who use computers moderately at school tend to have somewhat better learning outcomes than students who use computers rarely." But here was the kicker: "Students who use computers very frequently at school do much worse, even after accounting for social background and student demographics" (OECD, 2015).

But the OECD didn't suggest that technology be ditched from schools in light of this finding. "Technology is the only way to dramatically expand access to knowledge," said Andreas Schleicher, OECD director for education and skills. "To deliver on the promises technology holds, countries need to invest more effectively and ensure that teachers are at the forefront of designing and implementing this change" (OECD, 2015).

The key to tapping into the potential learning benefits of technology, it seems, rests in our hands as teachers. In Finland I saw my colleagues using technology on a regular basis, but in modest ways. One of the most common methods was the use of a "doc cam"—a simple piece of technology I've found in every Finnish school I've visited. Picture something that looks like an old-fashioned overhead projector, except that it's equipped with a miniature video camera.

On a nearly daily basis, I would observe teachers at my school using doc cams to provide visual aids while they were teaching. Not only that, but it was also a great way for students to communicate their learning to the class. For example, I'd often ask my students to demonstrate their solutions to math problems by using the doc cam at the front of our classroom. I'm not suggesting that every teacher go out and purchase one, just that the classroom technology that we use doesn't have to be sophisticated to be effective.

"I think the talk about technology in education has gotten way out of hand," Jere Linnanen, a middle school history teacher at Helsinki's Maunula Comprehensive School, told me. "[Education technology] can help you . . . but it's not about the tool. Or it shouldn't be about the tool."

Linnanen often uses the Google Classroom suite with his eighth and ninth graders to support the learning in his classroom, in which his students use the free software to create slide shows and documents together. He calls these tools "basic," but he finds that they're working well for his students. As a former executive at a Finnish educational technology start-up with an international reach, Linnanen has closely followed the technology scene over the last few years:

[Politicians] want education to be a problem that can be solved top down. They want to be able to say that, "If we put this much money into education technology, then we get these results. And we want to move up [in] the rankings so we press this button." But I think it should be more like bottom up, like grass

roots, like teachers connecting [with] teachers, sharing stuff, and connecting to their students. That's
where the focus should be.

Technology integration, when it supports learning, can
bring joy to teachers and students, especially when it allows
us to do what educator Will Richardson (2016) calls "the
extraordinary":

To connect live or asynchronously with people from
all over the world. To publish stuff to a global audience. To make things, programs, artifacts, inventions
that can't be made in the analog world.

While it's relatively rare, in my experience, to find Finnish schools where technology is used to do "the extraordinary," I think the common practice of using technology to
support learning, rather than distract from it, is wise. For
years, Finland's schools have proved that their students can
master important content and skills without investing heav-
ily in the latest tech gadgets. I think it's an important lesson
for all educators. If we want to teach for mastery, let's put
tech in its rightful place, as a tool for learning.

Bring in the music

One of the first things I noticed when I visited Minna Räihä's sixth grade class at the Kalevala Comprehensive School
in Kuopio was a drum set in the back of the classroom, along
with a few other musical instruments. In the morning, I
shared with her students that my four-year-old son loved

drumming but I couldn't play a lick of it. Minna assured me that one of her students could teach me. Sure enough, right before heading to lunch with Minna's class, one of her sixth graders, a skillful drummer, graciously led me over to the drum set in the classroom. A small group of children formed a semicircle around us. First, the boy modeled the proper technique, involving the base drum, the snare drum, and the high hat. He handed me the drum sticks, and I sat on the stool. Initially I was overwhelmed, struggling to put those three elements together. But that sixth grader, and another one of his classmates, didn't give up on me. Like good teachers, they kept giving me pointers and exuding optimism, and eventually I got the hang of it. The small group of children cheered.

That day Minna showed me a professional-looking CD that she and her students helped to create. I was impressed. Minna explained that her sixth graders have a few extra music lessons each week, because her students had chosen, years earlier, to have a special emphasis on music studies. It was an arrangement I had seen at a couple of other Finnish public schools.

Although Minna's class had a special focus on learning music, I had observed something similar in "regular" classrooms at my Helsinki school. We had a large music classroom, where most instruments were kept, but I noticed that my Finnish colleagues would sometimes bring musical instruments into their classrooms. Occasionally I'd hear the pulse of a base drum coming from the sixth grade classroom next door.

In recent years, schools across America have cut back on the arts, leaving some students without any music instruction. This hasn't been the case in Finland. In my first year of teaching in Helsinki, I was shocked to find that my fifth graders had the same number of lessons of math as music: three hours, every week. I used to think it was a little funny to give so many hours to a "special" subject, but over time I've stumbled across research linking music training to academic success, and I no longer question this Finnish practice.

For example, in a 2014 study, involving hundreds of children from low-income homes, researchers found that music lessons can help such kids improve their literacy and linguistic skills. Nina Kraus, a researcher and a neurobiologist at Northwestern University, discussed this link at the American Psychological Association's 122nd Annual Convention: "Research has shown that there are differences in the brains of children raised in impoverished environments that affect their ability to learn. . . . While more affluent students do better in school than children from lower income backgrounds, we are finding that musical training can alter the nervous system to create a better learner and help offset this academic gap" (APA, 2014).

Music lessons, the researchers concluded, seem to strengthen how the nervous system handles noise in a bustling atmosphere, such as a schoolyard. Because of this improvement in brain functioning, the children may develop better memory and a greater ability to focus in the classroom setting, which will help them to communicate better (APA, 2014).

Although Finland's classrooms are easily able to reap the benefits of having more music in their class schedules, there are certain steps that any teacher can take to infuse their classrooms with more music, even if formal music lessons are no longer offered at school. The idea of bringing in a drum set or carrying in a dozen classical guitars (as I experienced in my Helsinki classroom) would be fun, but I don't think efforts to bring in more music need to be this extensive. Also, it would be difficult for teachers to justify focusing on musical instruction if the curriculum doesn't call for it. The best arrangement, I can imagine, involves integration: mixing music with academic instruction.

For example, with my Helsinki fifth graders, I brought hip-hop into my classroom when we studied the elements of a story (in English language arts) and the water cycle (in a science class). On YouTube, I've found many fun hip-hop videos, with lyrics that reinforce the learning in the classroom. Singing those songs together, while rhyming and keeping the beat, wasn't just a fun way to engage the curriculum: Kraus's research suggests to me that efforts like these can, in part, help students develop stronger neural connections and better language skills.

Anne-Marie Oreskovich, a musician, a math scholar, and the founder of Math Musical Minds, believes that integrating music into math lessons can improve academic learning. For younger children, she suggests the simple exercise of playing enjoyable music with a discernible rhythm: the kids keep the beat (while counting, forward and backward) with simple objects, such as spoons. This activity can strengthen the children's ability to recognize patterns, grasping the structure and sequencing of numbers. For older children, Oreskovich suggests letting them make strings of numbers and portray them as chords. "Music decomposes to math," said Oreskovich, "and math decomposes to music" (quoted in Schiff, 2016).

During one lesson when I was in high school, one of my English teachers played a Bruce Springsteen song, on a boom box, as we analyzed its lyrics. It was such a (relatively) small effort by the teacher, but I remember this particular lesson because it was unusually fun and engaging; the musical component breathed life into this assignment.

At the elementary level, I've heard of some teachers who use music to get their students to transition from one activity to another. Additionally, I've met American educators in the public school setting who have used music to teach their young students essential content, such as the names of the continents. In one Massachusetts elementary school, where I taught computer lessons for several months, I remember hearing different variations of the "Continents Song," sung by students and their teachers. (It was a delightful experience to hear these children singing in the computer lab, which happened spontaneously when I started a Google Maps lesson.) Their elementary school teachers had taught them the names of the continents set to different melodies from classic songs, such as "Three Blind Mice." Later, when I became a classroom teacher, their creativity inspired me to do the same with my first and second graders, and I firsthand saw that this was a fun way for my young students to learn something well.

As teachers, we don't need to shy away from the strategy *bring in the music*, even if we're not musically inclined. We can experiment with different arrangements that feel comfortable for us and our students and, ultimately, tap into the joys and academic benefits of incorporating music in the classroom.

Coach more

One of the first things I noticed in my Helsinki school's woodworking classroom was a little wooden sign that read "Learning by Doing." Every time I visited, I'd see this maxim put in practice. Students were happily busy, working on individual projects they found interesting and challenging. I found that my colleague, the woodworking teacher, was usually circulating around the classroom and coaching, meeting with students and offering feedback (Ferlazzo, in press).

I saw the same thing in the home economics classroom and the textiles classroom where children often sew and knit. I'm convinced that this group of former Finnish colleagues has subscribed to the "learning by doing" approach for years, and that this belief powerfully informs their teaching, in which they spend a significant portion of classroom instruction working like coaches.

Many adults know from firsthand experience that the best way to master something is through practice in a "real-world" setting. The problem is that classroom learning, traditionally speaking, hasn't looked this way. At school, children often learn about science through watching videos, reading nonfiction texts, and completing exercises, rather than designing and implementing their own experiments like actual scientists. The practice of coaching puts the ownership of the learning process in the right place, squarely on the shoulders of the learners.

I don't think teachers need to be teaching unique subjects, such as woodworking or home economics, to tap into the genius of the learning-by-doing philosophy. All that's needed, I've found, is a shift in our thinking and a subsequent shift to our teaching approach.

In my first year of classroom teaching in the Boston area, I heard a mantra from a mentor teacher that I've never forgotten: the person who does the work does the learning. When I recall that first year of teaching, I cringe. I used to talk until the cows come home, usually while sitting on the rug with my first graders. "I'm learning a lot this year," I told a veteran coteacher one afternoon (Ferlazzo, in press).

"Sure," she said, "but how much are the students learning?" Ouch. I knew that my students, sitting and listening on the rug most of the day, weren't learning much at all.

To reverse this, I knew I needed to give up the "sage on the stage" routine. So I started experimenting, beginning in American classrooms and then in Finnish classrooms, with the aim of getting my students to do more of the learning. Earlier, I mentioned how I once brought a stopwatch to class to help keep my mini lessons short. In just a few days, I found that those shorter lessons now felt comfortable, and my students were having significantly more time—after the mini lesson—to learn through doing (Ferlazzo, in press).

While I felt satisfied with this pedagogical shift, once I moved to Finland it felt insufficient. My Finnish colleagues, especially those who taught woodworking, home economics, and textiles, showed me the joys of giving children even *more* opportunities to learn through doing.

In Chapter 3 I described how I made a significant change

to how I would teach English language arts in Helsinki by letting my students spend most of the lessons working more like *real* writers. They'd look to me as an editor or, to put it another way, a coach. In the section about the strategy *leave margin*, I discussed how this particular practice of restructuring my sixth graders' language arts lessons helped to develop the autonomy of my students. Now, I'm investigating how this shift and other similar practices promote mastery.

Giving my Helsinki students more time to work like writers during language arts was a good start, but it was insufficient on its own. My teacher-friend Jere Linnanen told me that students often need a "push" to progress; otherwise, they'll stay at their current levels. For me, pushing looks like giving good feedback.

When I mention good feedback, I'm not talking about distributing stickers and shouting, "Way to go!" I'm referring to feedback that's specific, honest, and constructive. Through blogging, crafting articles, and book writing, I've personally seen the importance of good feedback. In my experience, professional editors limit their praise. They might mention one or two things that they appreciate about a work, but they spend most of their time naming what needs improvement. Initially, I felt a little offended. Wasn't the primary job of a writing coach to applaud?

Nowadays I embrace this methodology: by limiting praise, editors emphasize feedback that's specific, honest, and constructive. These days, I'm no longer crushed if I hear only a few words of positive feedback from an editor, because I know my "coach" and I share the same goal: we both want to produce a high-quality work *together.* I'm convinced that nurturing this kind of attitude in the classroom would help students to learn better.

The best way to improve, I've found, is through addressing weak spots, and that's exactly where coaching is needed. The good coach shines a light on the undeveloped areas of the learning and then offers adequate support to the learner—through modeling and good feedback, primarily. There *is* a place for praise in our classrooms, but I suspect that praise is not something that skillful teachers will need to work to incorporate in their classrooms. It's something they provide quite naturally, in my experience.

If you're like me and you want to develop as a coach, the structure of your lessons must accommodate this role. We need a framework that facilitates learning by doing and plenty of opportunities for good feedback. For me, that structure is something called the workshop model. While I've seen variations of this approach, it's composed of three basic parts: a mini lesson introducing the day's aim, active independent work, and group reflection on how students have progressed toward that particular aim. (Paula Havu, my former colleague, once told me that this was billed as the ideal lesson structure during her teacher-training program.)

I was an elementary teacher in the Boston area when I first heard about this model and started to implement it in my classroom. In hindsight, I didn't always maximize this approach, because I'd sometimes spend too much time on mini lessons and reflections. My students would have benefited from having more time to complete independent work. Giving children adequate time to work paves the way for good teacher feedback.

To guide student work and teacher feedback, our classrooms need clear, achievable goals. I've found that one of the most effective things we can do as teachers, which helps us and our students to stay focused on mastery, is to incorporate learning targets into our teaching on a regular basis. Educators Connie Moss and Susan Brookhart (2012) define a learning target as follows:

> A learning target is not an instructional objective. Learning targets differ from instructional objectives in both design and purpose. As the name implies, instructional objectives guide instruction, and we write them from the teacher's point of view. Their purpose is to unify outcomes across a series of related lessons or an entire unit. . . .
>
> Learning targets, as their name implies, guide learning. They describe, in language that students understand, the lesson-sized chunk of information, skills, and reasoning processes that students will come to know deeply. We write learning targets from the students' point of view and share them throughout today's lesson so that students can use them to guide their own learning. (p. 3)

In my experience, the workshop model works seamlessly with learning targets, because it puts the emphasis on kids learning by doing, which allows teachers to work like coaches.

How do you write a learning target? According to Moss and Brookhart (2012), the process begins with a teacher choosing a standard and boiling it down to an objective for a lesson or a set of lessons, to make it clear what the teacher wants the children to achieve in the classroom. The next step involves reframing the objective to reflect what the children themselves should seek to achieve in the classroom. Moss and Brookhart recommend that an educator follow several steps when designing learning targets. The most crucial, in my opinion, is deciding on a "performance of understanding" (p. 39), informed by the lesson's teaching objective. During this step, teachers think about what their students could do to prove that they've achieved the instructional objective for the lesson or set of lessons.

In their book *Learning Targets*, Moss and Brookhart offer an example from a sixth grade teacher who's teaching a math lesson on variability. The teacher has identified the following instructional objectives: "Students will explain how the element of chance leads to variability in a set of data," and "Students will represent variability using a graph" (p. 38). With those objectives in hand, the teacher crafts a learning target for the students: "We will be able to *see a pattern in graphs we make* about the number of chips in our cookies, and we will be able to *explain what made that pattern*" (p. 39, emphasis added). Thus, this teacher designed the lesson's learning target with a performance of understanding in mind.

In my experience, one of the things that students need, in order to hit a learning target in the classroom, is a clear example of what success looks like. Although it's tempting to just tell students the success criteria (it's *much* faster this way!), I've found that children produce higher-quality work when they "discover," or identify, the key ingredients on their own through studying exemplars. (In a way, this is a *start with freedom* approach.)

Here are two scenarios at the high school level, adapted from one of Moss and Brookhart's examples. In one scenario, an English teacher tells his students that they're going to learn how to write an effective thesis statement for a persuasive speech. He distributes a list of criteria. Then he announces that they will have the next thirty minutes to practice writing strong thesis statements for their speeches. "Good luck!" he says.

In the second scenario, an English teacher brings in a collection of thesis statements of varying degrees of quality; some appear hastily written and unintelligible, while others appear methodically written and eloquent. (These are examples she has borrowed and cited from different sources, written on her own, or saved from previous classes.) This teacher starts the lesson by saying that they're going to be learning how to write effective thesis statements. But instead of handing out the success criteria and letting her students loose, she points to a question on the whiteboard: "What are the ingredients of a strong thesis statement for a persuasive speech?"

She splits the class into several small groups and distributes copies of the different thesis statements to each group. She gives the groups five minutes to investigate this collection of examples, as they consider the question on the whiteboard. The teacher then calls everyone together and asks, "So, what are the ingredients of a strong thesis statement for a speech?" At this point, the teacher is already aware of several key criteria, which she has identified before class, but she wants her students to take ownership of their learning by "discovering" these ingredients. She can guide them during the discussion, if they're struggling to identify the most important components.

Through a short discussion, her students identify the most important elements of a strong thesis statement. Then, with a clear picture of what success looks like, guided by an appropriate learning target, they are ready to practice well as they aim to master this skill of writing a strong thesis statement—and this teacher is ready to coach them well.

"Learning targets make the difference, from a student's point of view, between complying with teachers' requests and pursuing their own learning," Moss and Brookhart write. "Students who pursue their own learning demonstrate increased motivation, learn more, and develop stronger metacognitive skills" (2012, p. 40).

Prove the learning

Finnish education is famous for its (relative) lack of standardized tests, but this reputation has led some to believe that Finland's teachers abstain from testing their students. In my experience, this just isn't the case. At the elementary level, for example, I've found that Finnish educators offer more summative assessments than what I'd expect to see in American schools. This phenomenon stems, I believe, from Finland's traditional system of grading, in which children, even in some primary grades, are given a number grade for each subject at the end of each semester. The grading scale

ranges from four, the lowest, to ten, the highest. This traditional grading system puts pressure on Finnish teachers to
average the scores of tests, in order to come up with justifi-
able number grades.

That being said, the tide of traditional testing and grading seems to be changing in this Nordic country. Finland's
newest national core curriculum, which was implemented in
the fall of 2016, deemphasizes number grades for elementary
school children, giving schools the opportunity to give nar-
rative feedback at the end of a marking period in lieu of number grades. Today, there's more of a push for formative
assessment in Finnish schools, too.

While I'm opposed to traditional grading systems (I've
often found that grades distract students from the joy of
learning simply for the sake of learning), I am a fan of getting students to prove their learning, because it's something
that develops mastery. At my Helsinki school, I would often
notice my Finnish colleagues making their own summative
assessments. They might use aspects of the end-of-unit tests
provided by the school's commercial curricula, but I rarely
noticed them making straight copies of black-line masters
and administering them to their students (something I was
in the habit of doing in America).

Customizing tests was an obvious effort by my Finnish
colleagues to align assessments more closely to the teaching
in their classrooms. And this strategy paved the way for
their students to prove their learning more effectively.

That wasn't the only thing I noticed: typically, I'd see my
colleagues applying a simple principle in their custom-made
assessments. My Helsinki mentor teacher was the first person
to open my eyes to this particular aspect of testing in Fin-

land. She said that she'd often ask her students, when answering exam questions, to *perustella*. Initially she wasn't sure how to translate this Finnish word into English, but after discussing the concept, we decided that it means "justify." On my mentor teacher's tests, she'd often ask her students to show what they know by providing evidence of their learning.

Sure enough, when I'd study my colleagues' customized tests in the teachers' workroom or the teachers' lounge, I kept seeing the same philosophy at work. This simple practice of getting students to prove their learning, by justifying their answers on assessments, is something that may partially explain Finland's consistently high PISA scores, in which fifteen-year-olds must think critically and creatively.

The concept of *perustella* is perhaps most easily seen in Finland's high school matriculation tests. Once Finnish students have passed the required courses for high school, they are allowed to sit for the national Matriculation Examination, which is arranged by the Matriculation Examination Board and administered simultaneously throughout all high schools. Before graduating from high school, students must pass at least four individual tests from this national examination. They can choose which tests to complete, with the exception of one assessment: evaluating a student's ability in a native language—Finnish, Swedish, or Sami (Sahlberg, 2015). In *Finnish Lessons 2.0* (2015), Pasi Sahlberg explains what makes Finland's Matriculation Examination unique among typical standardized assessments around the world:

The nature of these individual exams is to try to test students' ability to cope with unexpected tasks. Whereas the California High School Exit Examination . . . , for example, is guided by a list of potentially biased, sensitive, or controversial topics to be avoided, the Finnish examination does the opposite. Students are regularly asked to show their ability to deal with issues related to evolution, losing a job, dieting, political issues, violence, war, ethics in sports, junk food, sex, drugs, and popular music. Such issues span across subject areas and often require multidisciplinary knowledge and skills. (Chapter 1, loc. 1083)

Here's a collection of sample questions for the Matriculation Examination, provided by Sahlberg:

- *Native language:* "Media is competing for audiences—what are the consequences?"
- *Philosophy and ethics:* "In what sense are happiness, good life and well-being ethical concepts?"
- *Health education:* "What is the basis of dietary recommendations in Finland and what is their aim?" (Strauss & Sahlberg, 2014)

. . .

IN HELSINKI, INSPIRED BY MY FINNISH COLLEAGUES, I started to design end-of-unit (summative) assessments that centered on getting my students to prove their learning better through open-ended, challenging questions, which required them to think creatively and critically. In responses to these kinds of questions, I'd award my students points for providing pieces of evidence, showing their knowledge and understanding of a particular content area.

Once I made this shift in how I designed these assessments, I found that I had a much better grasp on whether or not my students had mastered content in a particular subject at the end of a unit. That's because the children in my classroom had to literally prove their learning, whereas in the past I think the questions on my summative tests were often too easy and too narrow for this to happen. Furthermore, these Finnish-style assessments gave my students the leeway to demonstrate more than just a basic level of understanding and knowledge on tests.

These summative evaluations were often demanding for my Helsinki students, but I found that many of them seemed proud of their critical, creative responses to these challenging, open-ended questions. Previously, I had rarely noticed my students expressing healthy pride for answering test questions.

Here are a few example questions from tests I designed in different sixth grade subjects:

- *Physics:* Explain how "earthing" works. In your explanation, refer to the term "lightning conductor." Write sentences and create a labeled diagram to support your explanation.

- *Geography:* What is the difference between a vegetation zone and a climate zone? Explain in words and create a diagram, if it supports your explanation.
- *History:* Why did people migrate to Finland? Explain your thinking.
- *Ethics:* On the first ethics exam, you wrote about one "ethical dilemma" you might face in your life. Now, choose one "democratic dilemma" to write about. This can be a conflict in the world that's either real or imagined, so it doesn't necessarily have to be a problem that you may face in your life. It could be something that you've heard about on the news, or used your imagination to make up. Provide one specific example of a "democratic dilemma" and then, explain why it's a "democratic dilemma" with sentences.
- *Chemistry:* Imagine that you have been asked to find out whether toothpaste is acidic or alkaline. Thinking like a scientist, what would you do?

If we teachers want to further promote mastery in our classrooms, I think we need to do what I've noticed Finnish educators doing when designing custom-made exams: get students to justify their answers to difficult, open-ended questions. This strategy of getting students to prove their learning can be applied not just when we're producing summative assessments but on a daily basis: in classroom discussions, in group work, and in formative assessments.

Discuss the grades

When I first stepped into Pekka Peura's classroom at Vantaa's Martinlaakso High School, I wasn't sure what I'd find. I had heard that this high school math teacher, with blond hair that nearly covered his ears, no longer administers any tests. His tenth grade students sat in small clusters throughout the room, looking relaxed.

If Pekka taught a mini lesson that morning, I didn't notice it. After introducing me and a couple of other visitors, he let his students loose, and they knew exactly what to do. Throughout the lesson, nearly all of the students had their notebooks open, along with their math textbooks, as they worked to master different areas of math. Pekka floated around the classroom, stopping often to confer with students.

I asked one tenth grade student to explain Pekka's system. How did everyone know what to do? This student showed me a reference guide, which revealed a selection of math concepts based on the curriculum. These concepts were organized from the most basic to the most advanced, and under each category of concepts was a list of math exercises to complete. Also, I found a key, which suggested which number grade a student could receive upon reaching a tier of math concepts.

In the back of the classroom, I found two boys wearing baseball caps working on computers. Sitting in an empty chair behind them, I noticed that they were watching a YouTube clip. But that video wasn't math related: it was an Ultimate Fight Club match. I was a little surprised that they didn't even *try* to hide this from me, and I asked one of them about this level of freedom. He told me that Pekka trusts them to do what they need to do. At that moment, the teenage boy told me, he didn't feel like doing math—he felt like surfing YouTube. The work he wasn't doing during the lesson could also be completed at home.

In Pekka's math classes, there's no homework, at least not in the traditional sense. A student in his math class could, hypothetically, avoid doing any homework during the entire seven-week period. But there's a natural consequence: that student would have much less time to solve problems and, subsequently, much less time to move from mastering the basic concepts to the most advanced ones.

For the last seven years, Pekka has developed this system in which his students are constantly assessing themselves. Once every six or seven weeks (the typical length of a high school marking period in Finland), his students will meet with him individually for a brief conference, for about five to ten minutes, in which they'll agree on a final grade together. Usually, the student first suggests a grade, and according to Pekka, it's normally an accurate representation of the student's progress. Pekka found that, once he implemented this sort of system, he didn't think it was any less accurate than the traditional method of assigning a grade through averaging test scores.

As a teacher, I'm most impressed with how Pekka has given his students more ownership of assessment and grading, two areas that have traditionally remained exclusively in the hands of educators. The previous section, which explored the strategy *prove the learning*, focused on the topic of assessment; this section shifts our gaze to the subject of grading and the powerful strategy of discussing grades with students.

. . .

AT MY FINNISH PUBLIC SCHOOL, I'D OVERHEAR SEVERAL
of my colleagues, before publishing their report cards at the
end of a semester, having conversations with each of their
students about grades. These communications were typically brief. A teacher would share the grade she planned to
assign a child, and then that student would have an opportunity to respond. I found this practice to be incredibly
respectful. Not only were these teachers communicating
clearly with their students and strengthening rapport, but
they were also inviting these children to reflect on their
own learning.

Reflecting on learning needs to happen in our classrooms
before report cards, but I think this simple practice I observed
in Finland, communicating grades to students and inviting
their response, is essential. I've found that, at the end of a
marking period, most students—even the ones who seem to
have little interest in this thing called reflection—seem
ready to take a step back and assess their progress. Grades,
as arbitrary as they can sometimes seem to us as teachers,
often appear to mean a lot to children. For that reason, report
card season is a great time to seize the opportunity and help
students reflect on their learning.

I've *never* liked grading. Specifically, I've often felt that
handing out numbers has the potential to greatly diminish
the joyful classroom environment I'm trying to cultivate.
One major problem is that many students appear to tether
their self-esteem to the grades they receive: good grades,
smart kid; bad grades, dumb kid. As adults, we know that's
ridiculous—of course grades shouldn't define you.

But grading, at least for many of us teachers, is a problem that we just can't avoid. I confess that, in my classroom teaching, I've often dealt with this issue poorly, even after seeing good examples from my Finnish colleagues. Often I wouldn't feel comfortable discussing grades with my Helsinki students, so I'd rarely initiate conversations with them. I'd assign grades, print out report cards, administer them to my students, and hope that they wouldn't be too upset with the final numbers.

I wonder how much of my own experience as a student in American public and private schools has affected my thinking about grading as a teacher. In all my years of schooling in the United States, I can't remember a single instance in which a teacher took one minute to individually discuss my grades with me. I think it would have been relatively easy to arrange (during independent work in the classroom, for example), but somehow I can't recall it ever happening. What I do remember, though, is discussing grades with my parents, which seemed, in hindsight, good yet insufficient. I think I would have benefited greatly from having quick conversations with my teachers.

In the future, I want to do a better job of discussing grades with my students. Pekka Peura and other Finnish teachers have shown me why it's such a worthwhile endeavor, even if it feels uncomfortable. Through private discussions, we can provide our students with more understanding and ownership of their grades. It's a strategy that helps them to reflect on their learning and, ultimately, supports them as they seek to achieve mastery in our classrooms.

Mind-set

DESPITE THE TYPICAL CHALLENGES OF TEACHING in the United States, where school hours are relatively long, state standards are usually prescriptive, and standardized testing (and other demands) add considerable stress, I've met many American teachers who are brimming with passion for their work. Instead of seeing their professions just as jobs, they regard them as vocations.

Admittedly, one of the things I miss most about teaching in the United States is a vast community of purpose-driven teachers who are passionate about their craft. In my experience, it's common to find American educators who are so devoted to their professional growth that, every year, they spend a substantial amount of their own money and their free time on professional learning. This reality contrasts somewhat with what I've seen in Finland.

As I've visited different schools in Finland, I've seen many competent, hard-working teachers, who seem astute as professional problem solvers. One of the things I haven't observed, however, is a large number of Finnish educators who take intentional, voluntary steps to improve significantly as practitioners, whether it be through reading professional literature of their choice, attending summer institutes, or implementing new pedagogies in their classrooms. In Finland, I think I may have stumbled upon a cultural difference, which doesn't just concern the teaching profession. Over the years, I've spoken with a number of Finns, in different professional fields, who seem to embrace the motto "work to live" rather than "live to work." These individuals appear content with their jobs, but during their free time, they seem to prefer to pursue their own hobbies rather than making sizeable investments in their professional growth.

While I've seen many devoted American teachers who work with a strong sense of purpose, I do wonder about their approach for carrying out their calling. So far in this book, we've explored four different ingredients of happiness: well-being, belonging, autonomy, and mastery. But the fifth ingredient, mind-set, is perhaps the most crucial in terms of fostering a joyful classroom.

There are two predominant types of worldviews that people bring to life, according to happiness researcher Raj Raghunathan. "One extreme is a kind of scarcity-minded approach, that my win is going to come at somebody else's loss, which makes you engage in social comparisons," he said in a 2016 interview with *The Atlantic*'s Joe Pinsker. "And the other view is what I would call a more abundance-oriented approach, that there's room for everybody to grow."

The researcher points to children as being models of people who adopt the abundance-oriented approach because "extrinsic yardsticks" fail to sidetrack them (Pinsker, 2016). Kids pursue whatever offers them a significant amount of joy, Raghunathan said in the interview.

In Finland, I've met many teachers who seem to adopt this abundance-oriented approach. They seem unfazed by how they stack up to other teachers, and that attitude infuses their work with a sense of joy. One of the clearest signs of this mind-set in action is the significant amount of collaboration I've seen in Finnish schools. Even with the fifteen-minute breaks and the shorter school days, I doubt I would have seen Finnish educators collaborating very much if they viewed one another as competitors.

In the United States, the scarcity-minded approach might be a common one among educators. For example, I've lost count of how many times I've heard the term *master teacher* used to describe an American educator. Often I've wondered if the use of this title is less about describing a teacher's skillfulness and more about declaring a person's superiority. Surely there are "master teachers" in Finland, but I haven't heard anyone elevating them as such.

While Twitter may not be the best barometer, I'm fascinated by how many times I've seen American educators craft their short bios so that the focus, it seems, is on their accolades rather than their passions. Furthermore, "microcredentials" appear to be growing in popularity among American teachers, in which individuals receive digital badges that can be displayed on social media accounts for demonstrating mastery over particular aspects of teaching. While this kind of microcredentialing seems like a nice gesture of recognizing teachers for their strengths, I fear that it could be another form of professional posturing.

These are small, subtle pieces of evidence, but they suggest to me that many teachers in the United States bring a scarcity-minded approach to their work. If this is truly the case, Raghunathan suggests that this is a major problem: "The recipe for leading a life of happiness and fulfillment ultimately boils down to weaning oneself away from scarcity orientation, and toward abundance orientation" (2016, p. 242).

To increase the joy in our classrooms, we teachers need to cultivate an abundance-oriented approach. That doesn't mean tossing aside our strong sense of purpose—it means shifting our viewpoint away from competition, in which we no longer seek to be better than others, and instead focusing on being the best that we can be, regardless of how fellow educators are progressing.

This chapter is composed of six strategies for fostering an abundance-oriented worldview in our teaching, all of which are inspired by how I've observed Finnish educators approaching their work: *seek flow, have a thicker skin, collaborate over coffee, welcome the experts, vacate on vacation,* and *don't forget joy.*

Seek flow

In the Boston area, I once worked with a young teacher who preferred to keep the hallway space outside of her classroom covered with her students' work. There was no bulletin board in that section of the hallway, but that didn't deter her. She'd usually stick dozens of sheets of paper to the walls. Often I'd pass her classroom and feel a twinge of resentment. My classroom's bulletin board was just around the corner, where only a few people in the school would normally walk, and there I'd display only a few student creations.

As pathetic as this sounds today, I grew bitter toward this teacher. As I walked through the hallway, I started to think that all of her students' sheets of paper suggested that I was an inferior educator. But the truth, I'd reason with my nose in the air, was that I was the superior teacher, because I was careful to put up only "high-quality" work on my bulletin board.

In hindsight, I can see how clearly my insecure attitude decreased the joy in my teaching. I'd bring those negative emotions, stemming from bitterness, into the classroom, and I'd put increasing pressure on myself to perform better than my colleague. Instead of feeling free to enjoy my work, I'd often get distracted by this exhausting task of striving for superiority.

Superiority is an attractive goal, notes Raj Raghunathan. Researchers have found that higher-status individuals experience higher self-esteem and a greater sense of autonomy in their lives, indicating that being "superior" can actually *increase* happiness levels. But this finding doesn't mean that it's worthwhile to seek superiority—that's because the *pursuit* of superiority will probably decrease your level of joy, according to Raghunathan. It would be wiser to seek something called "flow" (Raghunathan, 2016).

But what is flow? The positive psychologist Mihaly Csikszentmihalyi, commonly seen as the guru of flow, describes this mental state in the following way:

> Being completely involved in an activity for its own sake. The ego falls away. Time flies. Every action, movement, and thought follows inevitably from the previous one, like playing jazz. Your whole being is involved, and you're using your skills to the utmost. (quoted in Cherry, 2016b)

As a teacher, I savor this mental state, in which I feel happily lost doing challenging, interesting work with the students. But research suggests that flow doesn't just bring on nice feelings—achieving flow is something that can enhance performance and develop one's skills (Cherry, 2016a; Cherry, 2016b). In other words, you experience positive emotions while working efficiently toward mastery. Csikszentmihalyi suggests that there are several factors that happen alongside flow. A person who is achieving this mental state may be working on a task, for example, that is intrinsically satisfying, goal-directed, demanding, and yet feasible (Cherry, 2016a; Cherry, 2016b).

The experience of flow is fostered, too, when we're totally focused on the goal we're seeking to achieve (Cherry, 2016a; Cherry, 2016b). When I reflect on those times when I feel like I'm doing my best work as a teacher, it's when I feel least distracted. It's during writer's workshops, for example, when my students are happily engaged in independent work, while I'm conferring with a child without any interruptions. Typically I've needed to coach my students to work in a focused way, so I can give my full attention to my teaching. As many experienced teachers know, a classroom environment where children do successful work independently doesn't happen magically.

If we want *everyone* in our classroom to achieve flow, minimizing obvious distractions (such as cell phones and chattiness) is essential. Crafting a short list of rules, with your students, could help in this regard. But one of the biggest distractions I've needed to prune is something hidden: a culture of competition.

In the Boston area, caring about being the "superior" teacher distracted me from doing my best work. I'd spend valuable time and energy worrying about proving myself instead of seeking flow. These days I think I've become more abundance oriented in my approach toward teaching. In Finland, I've met many teachers who don't seem interested in being superior. Simply put, they're quite happy to be competent in their work, and this noncompetitive mind-set seems to help them work better together. Also, I think it helps them to achieve flow on a regular basis.

Being teachers who seek flow, not superiority, is something that's not just good for us; it's also good for our students. Our students are watching us, and if they see that we're seeking to do our best work, free of comparing ourselves to others, I'm confident that this kind of example will foster a noncompetitive culture in our classrooms. We want our children to experience flow on a regular basis, and minimizing the major distraction of competition is crucial. This positive change we want to see— as is so often the case in teaching—starts with us.

Have a thicker skin

During my two years of teaching in Helsinki, I was grateful to have a terrific mentor teacher, who always seemed willing to meet with me—even when it was unexpected. Once, we had a parent–teacher night early in the fall, and I was swarmed by parents in the hallway. My mentor teacher stood by, watching silently until the last parent waved goodbye. Then she opened her mouth, and her words caught me by surprise: she wondered, aloud, if I was too accommodating with parents.

Initially I was a little defensive. I had always prided myself on communicating well with parents, and I didn't think I was doing anything wrong that evening. I can't recall exactly what I had said in those hallway conversations, but my mentor suggested that I seemed too eager to please. My Finnish colleague explained that, in some conversations with parents, she would communicate the following message: you're the expert at home, and I'm the expert at school. My colleague told me that since I was a professional, I should start seeing myself that way. I should have a thicker skin, she suggested. Like Kevlar.

My mentor's boldness surprised me. Before this interaction, I had talked with many teachers about the occasional challenges of working with parents, but I'd never seen such mental toughness on display. In my previous conversations with American teachers, I sensed that the "difficult" parents intimidated them. (Historically, I've felt this way, too.) Two of the most popular methods for pacifying these parents seemed to be either flat-out accommodation or running and hiding.

That evening I began to grasp the importance of having a tough skin. Sometimes interactions with parents, students, and colleagues can be challenging, and it can be tempting to get discouraged, but that place of discouragement is where our happiness can quickly disappear. As teachers, we need to develop resilience to keep our classrooms joyful.

To be clear, having a tough skin is different from being obstinate. My mentor wasn't suggesting that I ignore the feedback of others but, instead, that I be confident in my expertise as a teacher. I was a professional, and I should carry myself in that way.

Much has been written about the importance to raising resilient (or "gritty") students, but I haven't seen too much literature on the importance of developing resilient teachers. Some of the most joyful teachers I know are some of the toughest—their confidence seems rooted in something beyond their performance. When these educators make mistakes, they bounce back quickly.

In Finland, many of my colleagues impressed me with how they'd deal with conflicts—with parents, fellow teachers, and even students. As teachers, it's not a matter of *if* we'll face issues in the workplace; it's a matter of *when*. Having a tough skin is something that helps protect the joy of teaching.

The Finnish word *sisu* might be celebrated more than any other word in this tiny Nordic country. It's a human attribute—usually attached to the people of Finland—that can be translated as "guts" or "bravery in the face of adversity." It's that same attitude of *sisu* I saw reflected in my mentor's words: you're a professional!

In Helsinki, I found myself developing more *sisu*. Being

the new guy at a new school in a foreign land didn't exactly make me immune to sharp feedback—I received my fair share. Often that feedback, though, prompted me to make useful changes to my work. But there were other instances in which I heard tough feedback, disagreed with it, and didn't make accommodations. That surely upset some people, but in the end I felt like I could handle the pushback. I was a professional, and I was seeking to do my best as a teacher. Having that thick skin helped me to keep my classroom joyful.

Specifically, having a tough skin means taking a deep breath when you receive a long, barbed e-mail from an upset parent and leaving it alone until *you* feel ready to address it. It means, too, not getting crushed when your principal publicly praises one of your colleagues but then doesn't recognize your similarly solid work. Also, it means not taking it personally when one of your students curses you to your face.

One of the practices I've adopted as a teacher, when I'm feeling especially overwhelmed by professional challenges, is setting aside time before I crawl into bed to journal about that day's concerns. Generally speaking, I don't sleep very well until I've identified these underlying issues and put them into perspective. I've noticed that often the words I've heard during that school day—from parents, colleagues, and students—can be the things that seem to gnaw at me the most. I'm not a regular journal keeper, but I've found that the simple act of sitting down to name those sources of anxiety can alleviate much of my stress. I'll sleep so much better, too.

Typically, I set up my journal in a very simple way by drawing a line down the middle of the page to create two columns. On one side I write "anxieties" and on the other side I write "realities." Then I'll spend the next few minutes recalling and jotting down as many things that bothered me about that school day under the anxieties column. Once I'm finished, I'll move onto the realities column, writing down a sentence or so to correspond with each anxiety.

This second column helps me to *not* blow that day's frustrations out of proportion. The idea is that I can see those anxieties for what they are, as objectively as possible. When I write a sentence of reality, I try to think positively about the frustration in the first column. I might even suggest an action I can take the next day at school. Here's an example:

Anxieties	**Realities**
Parent sent an e-mail criticizing our new biology unit.	Our new unit clearly aligns with the biology curriculum. Tomorrow, I can send that parent a brief message communicating this point.
Student accused me of overlooking bullying.	Bullying is a serious issue, but I've yet to observe it in our classroom. In the morning, I'll speak with this student, just to listen, and then I'll decide what to do next.

Journaling in this way is a useful intervention when you feel discouraged as a teacher, but a helpful ongoing practice involves exercising gratitude. I've found that the simple act of giving thanks, publicly and privately, is something that sustains me, in the good and the bad times of teaching. Sonja

Lyubomirsky of the University of California, Riverside refers to "gratitude" as a "metastrategy" because, in the words of Raj Raghunathan (2016, p. 77), "it helps boost happiness in many different ways." A handful of studies, for example, reveal that giving thanks fortifies relationships (Raghunathan, 2016).

The exercise of giving thanks is a practice that diminishes the harmful desire to pursue superiority—that's because, according to Raghunathan, it "hinges on the idea that no one achieves anything just by themselves" (2016, p. 77).

Collaborate over coffee

For this book, I interviewed several Finnish teachers—at different levels, in different schools—to hear more about their classroom experiences and gain their professional insights. There were two questions I'd ask in each of these interviews: "What brings you joy as a teacher, and what brings your students joy?"

One of the most popular answers I heard from Finnish teachers, regarding what brings them joy, is collaboration. This result doesn't exactly surprise me. Here's a short excerpt from my essay in the book *Flip the System: Changing Education from the Ground Up* (Elmers & Kneyber, 2016):

In Finland, I found a school structure that fostered rich collaboration among teachers. In nearly 50 percent of my lessons, I was paired with one or two of my colleagues. Teachers in my school were not just collaborating in the traditional sense, by planning and teaching lessons together—they were truly laboring together, sharing the burdens of teaching with each other. They were helping each other track down the resources they'd need for an upcoming lesson. They were discussing better ways to support needy students. They were analyzing the curriculum together. They were talking about how to improve recess for the kids. They were grading tests together. They were offering tech support to each other. To my surprise, this work often happened in between sips of coffee, during those fifteen-minute breaks throughout the day. (pp. 176–177)

Researchers Andy Hargreaves and Dennis Shirley (2012) also noticed this collaborative atmosphere in Finnish schools:

Teachers in Finland cooperate as a matter of habit, not just to complete assigned tasks. . . . Cooperation is not just an add-on when the workday is over. It's not about temporary teamwork or interpreting student achievement data together after busy days at school. Cooperation is about how they create curriculum and how the work itself gets done. A ministry official explained: "If you give resources to them, they find a way to solve the problem." Vision and goals in Finnish schools are often implicit and shared through daily acts of cooperation, rather than just set out in a printed strategic plan. (p. 51)

Over the years, I've gotten the sense that teachers in the United States want to work together, like so many Finnish teachers are in the habit of doing. They understand the rationale for more cooperation, but they feel like their busy schedules are holding them back.

As teachers who want to experience the joys and benefits of collaboration, I think it's wise for us to focus on something we have more control over: adopting a different mind-set. Finnish educators benefit from a lighter schedule (with frequent fifteen-minute breaks and shorts days), but I've concluded that the reason they collaborate so frequently is that they don't view collaboration as a luxury. Instead, they see it as a necessity.

As I described earlier, I had the privilege of coteaching about half of my lessons during my first year of teaching in Helsinki—but, surprisingly, I spent most of that year doing little coplanning. Resource teachers would come by my classroom, lend a hand, and then leave. I didn't possess a mind-set in which I welcomed cooperation during my free time—I saw this kind of joint work as slightly inconvenient, and if I'm honest, I thought I was just fine on my own.

But it was during that second year when I relied on my colleagues more often. One of the major reasons for this stemmed from a crisis I experienced in the fall, in which I felt very discouraged as a teacher. Throughout that second year, several of my colleagues lifted me up though collaboration, and in my opinion, it ended up being a terrific year. I largely credit them for this triumph.

The shift in my mind-set happened when I believed I was a better teacher when I relied more on my colleagues. With this strategy, *collaborate over coffee*, I'm recommending that teachers start looking for casual, "natural" ways of working with fellow teachers. While many teachers have benefited from working with other teachers online (myself included) through Twitter and other social media platforms, I think we need to get back to doing more of the old-fashioned form

of collaboration: face-to-face interactions with our colleagues. Indeed, these are the people that we see every day,
and just as we thrive when our coworkers support us, those
same coworkers thrive when we support them—it's a two-
way street.

I used to think collaboration had to be something serious
and structured. I had this mental image of teachers putting
their heads together, looking exhausted, as they pored over
unit plans. Generally speaking, I rarely experienced this
kind of collaboration at my Finnish school. Typically, collaboration seemed to happen organically—and often in the
teachers' lounge.

Nowadays, I define collaboration, in the school context,
as anything that two or more people do together to enhance
the quality of teaching and learning. So that means that a
two-minute conversation about how to respond respectfully
to a parent's e-mail would count as collaboration. So, too,
would a five-minute chat about how to accommodate the
learning needs of a struggling student.

More than anything, I think collaboration is all about
mind-set. If you truly believe that you are a better teacher
when you're working in concert with others, then I think
you will quite naturally find small, simple ways of collaborating. I don't think my colleagues in Helsinki had to work
hard to collaborate. Their work together seemed like a by-
product of their teaching mind-set.

To collaborate better, cultivating that "us" attitude is
important, but so too is the frequency in which you're checking in with your colleagues. In the beginning of this book, I
described how three of my Finnish colleagues, after one
month of school, told me that they were concerned that I

wasn't spending enough time in the teachers' lounge. One of these teachers told me she *needed* to pay a daily visit to the lounge, where she would slow down and reconnect with others. When I started to visit the lounge more often, I found that the simple act of sitting down for a few minutes with my colleagues (typically on a daily basis) paved the way for greater collaboration.

Welcome the experts

While I taught in Helsinki, I noticed that my Finnish colleagues seemed to invite one another's classes into their classrooms somewhat regularly. These gestures were often small, but they seemed meaningful, bringing joy to them and their students.

Once, one of the physics teachers invited my class into one of the middle school science labs for an introductory lesson on electricity. Graciously, he taught this lesson during one of his free blocks. On another occasion, I was teaching a lesson on the pH scale, and I hoped to use the same lab. After school, another of my middle school colleagues helped me to prepare materials. That afternoon, she also taught me a little lesson on chemical compounds, which I used the following day.

When I felt uncomfortable about teaching a biology unit on sex, a female colleague volunteered to host a private Q&A with my female students in her classroom, while I met with my male students. Beforehand, she helped me to set up a question box, where the children could ask anonymous questions about sex. Later, the same colleague invited me into her classroom, where I shared about my experiences living in the United States. Her students were studying the concept of budgeting and seemed shocked to hear that, during my last year of living in the Boston area, one-third of my gross income went toward paying for health insurance.

Predictably, I wasn't comfortable with the practice of welcoming my colleagues into my classroom until I had seen this strategy modeled. But by the end of my second year of teaching in Helsinki, I had become a convert. I invited several of my colleagues into my classroom throughout the year, and they spent hours of their time investing in my students' learning. Sometimes they visited during their regular teaching hours, while on other occasions they came during their free time. It wasn't difficult to arrange—ultimately, all I needed to do was invite them.

I found that the more I welcomed experts into my classroom, the more I began to view myself as a resource manager who could design great learning experiences for my class by tapping into talents outside of my own. This new way of thinking took pressure off of my shoulders, because I didn't need to be some jack-of-all-trades.

If we teachers want to combat this scarcity-minded worldview, I think we need to start recognizing and benefiting from the expertise of others (inside and outside our school communities). The strategy *welcome the experts* affirms the abundance-oriented worldview.

Inviting your colleagues into your classroom, I've found, is a good starting point. And given that you work together in the same building, it should be fairly easy to arrange. From the examples I provided earlier, you know that this kind of collaboration doesn't need to be anything elaborate. Perhaps you have a colleague who has visited Mexico before and you're teaching a unit on that country. Could you ask that teacher to share a few photos from her trip and a few insightful stories? Or perhaps you want your students to keep a journal, and you have a colleague who's a passionate writer, who has been filling notebooks with his own thoughts for years—you could ask him into the classroom to talk about the benefits of journaling and share his advice on how to get started.

While welcoming other colleagues into your classroom may seem like an unnecessary extra, I think you'll find that it's worth the small effort. If you're concerned about one another's time, consider a "teacher swap": while a teacher is serving as the expert in your classroom, you could serve as the expert in that colleague's classroom. Once, two of my Helsinki colleagues exchanged roles in this way: the first grade classroom teacher, Paula Havu, switched places with a fifth grade classroom teacher. I spoke with Paula about this experience, and she recalled it wistfully.

Welcoming fellow teachers (and other experts, such as parents) into your classroom sends a message to your students that you're looking to learn from others. And if you're like me, cultivating this type of attitude makes it easier to view students as experts, too. I asked Paula to describe what brings children joy in the classroom, and she spoke to the importance of giving kids more ownership by letting them teach sometimes. "They are experts in many areas, so using them more in the classroom instead of you being the leader . . . the kids get more excited, they have choice."

Before coming to Finland, I had embraced the idea of bringing experts into the classroom, but my vision, I admit, was quite narrow. Often I'd overlook the experts within the walls of my school building. During my first year in Hel-

sinki, if you recall, I spent a significant amount of effort getting Finnish Olympic and Paralympic athletes to visit during
those first weeks of school. In hindsight, it would have been
much more efficient if I first tapped into the resources within
my school community. These days, I still believe that welcoming experts outside the school can be valuable, but I
think it's best to start by considering the people around you.
Not only will their contributions benefit your classroom, but
also it's likely that your invitation will affirm their expertise—it's a win-win.

Vacate on vacation

When I accepted the job of teaching fifth graders in Helsinki, I was ecstatic. But I was also tentative. I had a million
questions about how to teach well in Finland.

My Finnish principal must have guessed that I'd be brimming over with queries, because she told me that she'd be
away on something called a summer holiday until late July.
The principal's unavailability surprised me slightly, because
the principals I'd known in America seemed to work throughout the entire summer. The Finnish principal graciously suggested that I contact a Finnish colleague with my questions.

So I e-mailed this fellow teacher and asked to speak with
her the following week on the phone, and then another curious thing happened: I didn't hear from this colleague until
July, and when she e-mailed me, she politely suggested that
we chat *after* the holiday, saying something about her summer cottage. A pattern was emerging. It seemed that my Helsinki coworkers were literally vacating during the summer.

Initially I was skeptical of this approach. The American

educators I had grown to respect never seemed to stop working just because school was out for the summer. I used to do
the same thing. In the United States, I'd often spend a large
portion of the summer attending teaching seminars, reading
professional literature, and conducting home visits where I'd
meet with parents and students. I loved the summer holiday,
because I had more free time to do work. However, in Finland, where teachers are often depicted in the international
media as top-notch, I found scores of educators who disconnected for the majority of the summer. Today, I've grown to
appreciate this popular practice among the Finns.

For years, setting aside a significant period of time for
rest and relaxation each summer wasn't a priority of mine,
but these days I've found that I thrive from having longer
stretches of time to recharge. It's what helps me to prepare
for another school year. In my experience, I've found that
Finland's educators do very little school-related work during their summer holidays, generally speaking, but even
after a few years of living in this Nordic country, I confess
that this approach feels too extreme for me. I'm in favor of a
hybrid approach, in which there's a healthy chunk of time for
disconnecting and a healthy chunk of time for professional
development during the long break. As a teacher, I've found
that there's no better time than summer months to reflect on
my work and encounter new inspiring ideas I can incorporate into my classroom.

The problem I've detected among American educators is
that we sometimes neglect to leave sufficient time for
recharging during the summer. Catching up on sleep and
reading interesting books are good basic things, but so too
is this Finland-inspired strategy of setting aside sufficient

time to *vacate on vacation*. As I hinted before, I'm not proposing that teaching-related work go completely untouched for
the entire summer. Rather, I'm suggesting that we teachers
prioritize designated stretches of putting work aside.

In her book *Overwhelmed*, Brigid Schulte (2014) described
a compelling study, conducted by Harvard Business School,
which seems to bolster the case for taking adequate time off:

> [The researchers] compared two groups of workers
> at a Boston consulting firm. One group worked fifty
> or more hours a week, didn't use all their vacation
> time, and were constantly tethered to the office with
> electronics. The other group worked forty hours,
> took full vacations, and coordinated time off and
> after-hours on-call time so clients' needs could be
> covered but people could regularly, predictably, and
> without guilt totally unplug from the office. Which
> group produced better work? The team with time off,
> not surprisingly, reported higher job satisfaction and
> better work-life balance. But they also increased
> learning, improved communication with their team,
> worked more efficiently, and were ultimately more
> productive than their ideal worker colleagues. Other
> studies have found that employees who take full vaca-
> tions are not only more likely to stay with the firm
> but also receive higher performance reviews, and that
> workers are not only more creative but that turning
> off the constant barrage of e-mails and the ideal
> worker requirement to respond to them immediately
> enables people to concentrate and get more done with
> less stress. (p. 91)

I think it's wise, if you can afford it, to physically vacate with your family, with friends, or on your own during the summer, fleeing to the hills for a day trip, going on a cruise, relaxing on the beach for a few days, and so forth. That being said, I don't think it's absolutely necessary to get away to reap the benefits of a vacation. What matters most is our mind-set. In other words, it's possible to "go on a vacation" but not actually vacate, because you've brought your work along with you. (I know this, because I've tried it before; those "vacations" weren't refreshing.)

What's helpful, I've found, is when I embrace that summer holiday mind-set (the one I've seen so often applied in Finland) and set aside a few days, or weeks, to stay off e-mail and social media, especially during the summer. It's something that has encouraged me to be more physically active, more appreciative of nature, more rested, and more present with my family and friends.

Don't forget joy

Around the world, there appears to be a growing movement to prioritize happiness in schools. Alejandro Adler, while pursuing a PhD in positive psychology at the University of Pennsylvania, ran a study of eighteen schools, involving more than eight thousand secondary students, in the country of Bhutan. Classrooms implemented either a happiness curriculum, which emphasized ten nonacademic life skills like mindfulness, interpersonal relationships, and self-awareness, or a placebo curriculum (Adler, 2015; Parker, 2016).

The study indicated that student well-being and standardized test scores were significantly boosted by the happiness curriculum. "Well-being and academic achievement seem not to be antagonistic, as some have suggested," wrote Adler (2015). "On the contrary, increased well-being raised academic achievement."

In 2016, Finnish comprehensive schools implemented Finland's newest core curriculum, where joy is being prioritized as a learning concept. What I love about this simple gesture is that it's exactly the kind of thing that, research suggests, can boost happiness.

In an experiment conducted by Raj Raghunathan (2016), one group of workers got a daily e-mail for one week suggesting that they make choices to increase their level of happiness, and when that week concluded, that group said they were much happier than those employees who didn't get the e-mail. Through that study and others, Raghunathan found that when people receive a reminder on a daily-basis to maximize happiness, they make tiny decisions that contribute to greater happiness in their lives (Pinsker, 2016).

This book's most important strategy is probably the simplest: *Don't forget joy.* On difficult days (everyone has them), it might be tempting to forget about prioritizing joy in our classrooms. We might feel like caving in to the unreasonable demands of some pushy parents, or prodding our kids to work nonstop without breaks, or rushing ahead without celebrating student learning. Chances are, given the difficult situations that many American teachers face in this age of test-based accountability, it may be easier to *not* prioritize joy in our classrooms.

But it's joy that keeps me going as a teacher, and I'm committed—whether I'm teaching in Finland, the United States, or somewhere else in the world—to remember it and prioritize it in my classroom. How about you?

References

Adler, A. (2015, April 30). Gross national happiness and positive education in Bhutan. *IPEN Blog.* Retrieved October 20, 2016, from http://www.ipositive-education.net/gross-national-happiness-and-positive-education-in-bhutan/

Allen, J. G., MacNaughton, P., Satish, U., Santanam, S., Vallarino, J., & Spengler, J. D. (2016). Associations of cognitive function scores with carbon dioxide, ventilation, and volatile organic compound exposures in office workers: A controlled exposure study of green and conventional office environments. *Environmental Health Perspectives, 124*(6), 805–812. http://dx.doi.org/10.1289/ehp.1510037

Anderson, M. (2010). *The well-balanced teacher: How to work smarter and stay sane inside the classroom and out.* Alexandria, VA: ASCD.

APA (American Psychological Association). (2014, August 8). Musical training offsets some academic achievement gaps, research says. *Science Daily.* Retrieved September 22, 2016, from https://www.sciencedaily.com/releases/2014/08/140808110024.htm

Cherry, K. (2016a, March 15). Five ways to achieve flow. *Very Well.* Retrieved October 20, 2016, from https://www.verywell.com/ways-to-achieve-flow-2794769

Cherry, K. (2016b, May 6). What is flow? *Very Well.* Retrieved

October 20, 2016, from https://www.verywell.com/what-is -flow-2794768

Cheryan, S., Ziegler, S. A., Plaut, V. C., & Meltzoff, A. N. (2014). Designing classrooms to maximize student achievement. *Policy Insights from the Behavioral and Brain Sciences, 1*(1), 4–12. http:// dx.doi.org/10.1177/2372732214548677

Connelly, C. (2016, January 3). Turns out monkey bars and kickball might be good for the brain. *National Public Radio.* Retrieved October 19, 2016, from http://www.npr.org/sections/ed/2016/01 /03/460254858/turns-out-monkey-bars-and-kickball-are-good -for-the-brain

Davis, L. C. (2015, August 31). When mindfulness meets the class-room. *The Atlantic.* Retrieved October 20, 2016, from http:// www.theatlantic.com/education/archive/2015/08/ mindfulness-education-schools-meditation/402469/

Deruy, E. (2016, May 20). Does mindfulness actually work in schools? *The Atlantic.* Retrieved October 20, 2016, from http:// www.theatlantic.com/education/archive/2016/05/ testing-mindfulness-in-the-early-years/483749/

Elmers, J., & Kneyber, R. (Eds.). (2016). *Flip the system: Changing edu-cation from the ground up.* London: Routledge.

Ferlazzo, L. (2016, August 8). Response: starting the new year by 'building relationships'. *Education Week Teacher.* Retrieved on October 23, 2016, from http://blogs.edweek.org/teachers/ classroom_qa_with_larry_ferlazzo/2016/08/response_ starting_the_new_year_by_building_relationships.html

Ferlazzo, L. (in press). *Education Week Teacher.*

Finnish National Board of Education. (2016). *National core curriculum for basic education 2014.* Helsinki: Next Print.

Fisher, A. V., Godwin, K. E., & Seltman, H. (2014). Visual environ-ment, attention allocation, and learning in young children: when too much of a good thing may be bad. *Psychological Science 25*(7), 1362–1370.

Halinen, I. (2015, March 25). What is going on in Finland? Curriculum reform 2016. Retrieved October 20, 2016, from http://www.oph.fi/english/current_issues/101/0/what_is_going_on_in_finland_curriculum_reform_2016

Hargreaves, A., & Shirley, D. (2012). *The global fourth way: The quest for educational excellence* [Kindle Reader version]. Retrieved from Amazon.com

Higgins, J. (2015, December 10). Buildings with fresher air linked to better thinking. *Seattle Times.* Retrieved October 20, 2016, from http://www.seattletimes.com/education-lab/buildings-with-fresher-air-linked-to-better-thinking/

Hoffman, J. (2014, June 9). Rethinking the colorful kindergarten classroom. *Well.* Retrieved October 20, 2016, from http://well.blogs.nytimes.com/2014/06/09/rethinking-the-colorful-kindergarten-classroom/?_r=0

Jennings, P. A. (2015). *Mindfulness for teachers: Simple skills for peace and productivity in the classroom.* New York: Norton.

Khamsi, R. (2016, May 15). Bullies have a trump card. *Slate.* Retrieved October 20, 2016, from http://www.slate.com/articles/health_and_science/science/2016/05/anti_bullying_programs_might_not_work_as_well_for_popular_bullies_like_donald.html

Khazan, O. (2016, July 21). How noise pollution impairs learning. *The Atlantic.* Retrieved October 20, 2016, from http://www.theatlantic.com/health/archive/2016/07/toddlers-and-noise/492164/

Lemov, D. (2015). *Teach like a champion 2.0: 62 techniques that put students on the path to college* [Kindle Reader version]. Retrieved from Amazon.com

Liikkuva Koulu. (n.d.). More active and pleasant school days, brochure. Retrieved October 20, 2016, from http://www.

liikkuvakoulu.fi/filebank/2342-Liikkuvakoulu_yleisesite_
en_web.pdf

Louv, R. (2008). *Last child in the woods: Saving our children from
nature-deficit disorder.* Chapel Hill, NC: Algonquin Books.

Louv, R. (2011). *The nature principle: Human restoration and the
end of nature-deficit disorder.* Chapel Hill, NC: Algonquin
Books.

Miller, D. (2002). *Reading with meaning.* Portland, ME: Stenhouse.

Moss, C. M., & Brookhart, S. M. (2012). *Learning targets: Helping students aim for understanding in today's lesson.* Alexandria, VA: ASCD.

National Center for Children in Poverty. (2016). Child poverty.
Retrieved July 15, 2016, from http://www.nccp.org/topics/child-
poverty.html

OECD (Organization of Economic Cooperation and Development).
(2015, September 15). New approach needed to deliver on technology's potential in schools. Retrieved September 27, 2016, from
http://www.oecd.org/education/new-approach-needed-to-
deliver-on-technologys-potential-in-schools.htm

Parker, O. (2016, July 11). Should happiness be part of the school curriculum? *The Telegraph.* Retrieved October 20, 2016, from http://
www.telegraph.co.uk/education/2016/07/11/
should-happiness-be-part-of-the-school-curriculum/

Pellegrini, A. (2005, March 21). Give children a break. *Project Syndi-
cate.* Retrieved on October 27, 2016, from https://www.project-
syndicate.org/commentary/give-children-a-break

Pinsker, J. (2016, April 26). Why so many smart people aren't happy.
The Atlantic. Retrieved October 20, 2016, from http://www.the-
atlantic.com/business/archive/2016/04/why-so-many-smart
-people-arent-happy/479832/

Raghunathan, R. (2016). *If you're so smart, why aren't you happy?* [Kin-
dle Reader version]. Retrieved from Amazon.com

Richardson, W. (2016, July 12). The digital ordinary. Retrieved October 20, 2016, from http://willrichardson.com/the-digital-ordinary/

Ring, E. (2016, June 10). Anti-bullying programme focused on changing bystander behaviour should be in Irish schools. *Irish Examiner.* Retrieved October 20, 2016, from http://www.irishexaminer. com/ireland/anti-bullying-programme-focused-on-changing-bystander-behaviour-should-be-in-irish-schools-404099.html

Sage Publications. (2014, November 4). Researchers recommend features of classroom design to maximize student achievement [Press release]. Retrieved September 22, 2016, from https://us. sagepub.com/en-us/nam/press/researchers-recommend-features -of-classroom-design-to-maximize-student-achievement-0

Sahlberg, P. (2015). *Finnish Lessons 2.0: What can the world learn from educational change in Finland?* [Kindle Reader version]. Retrieved from Amazon.com

Schiff, S. (2016, July 11). A singing Harvard mathematician on using music to convince your kid they love math. *Fatherly.* Retrieved October 20, 2016, from https://www.fatherly.com/activities/ music-activities/how-to-teach-kids-math-using-music/

Schonert-Reichl, K. A., Oberle, E., Lawlor, M. S., Abbott, D., Thomson, K., Oberlander, T. F., & Diamond, A. (2015). Enhancing cognitive and socio-emotional development through a simple-to-administer mindfulness-based school program for elementary school children: A randomized control trial. *Developmental Psychology, 51*(1), 52–66.

Schulte, B. (2014). *Overwhelmed: Work, love, and play when no one has the time.* [Kindle Reader version]. Retrieved from Amazon.com.

Schwartz, K. (2014, October 6). Why daydreaming is critical to effective learning. *Mindshift.* Retrieved October 20, 2016, from https://ww2.kqed.org/mindshift/2014/10/06/why-daydreaming -is-critical-to-effective-learning/

Seppälä, E. (2016). *The happiness track: How to apply the science of happiness to accelerate your success* [Kindle Reader version]. Retrieved from Amazon.com

Strauss, V., and Sahlberg, P. (2014, March 24). The brainy questions on Finland's only high-stakes standardized test. *Washington Post.* Retrieved September 27, 2016, from https://www.washingtonpost.com/news/answer-sheet/wp/2014/03/24/the-brainy -questions-on-finlands-only-high-stakes-standardized-test/

Turner, S. (2013, October 18). TCU professor launches "pilot" program on recess at Starpoint School. *TCU 360.* Retrieved October 20, 2016, from https://www.tcu360.com/story/18744tcu -professor-launches-pilot-program-recess-starpoint-school/

Walker, T. (2014, June 30.) How Finland keeps kids focused through free play. *The Atlantic.* Retrieved on October 22, 2016, from http://www.theatlantic.com/education/archive/2014/06/ how-finland-keeps-kids-focused/373544/

Walker, T. (2015, January 9). Finnish schools are on the move— and America's need to catch up. *The Atlantic.* Retrieved October 20, 2016, from http://www.theatlantic.com/education/archive /2015/01/finnish-schools-are-on-the-moveand-americas -need-to-catch-up/384358/

Walker, T. (2016a, September 15). Kindergarten, naturally. *The Atlantic.* Retrieved on October 22, 2016, from http://www.theatlantic.com/education/archive/2016/09/ kindergarten-naturally/500138/

Walker, T. (2016b, October 7). The disproportionate stress plaguing American teachers. Retrieved on October 22, 2016, from http://www.theatlantic.com/education/archive/2016/10/ the-disproportionate-stress-plaguing-american- teachers/503219/

Walker, T. (2016c, September 29). The ticking clock of teacher burnout. *The Atlantic.* Retrieved on October 22, 2016, from http://
www.theatlantic.com/education/archive/2016/09/
the-ticking-clock-of-us-teacher-burnout/502253/

Walker, T. (2016d, September 1). Where sixth-graders run their own
city. *The Atlantic.* Retrieved on October 42, 2016, from http://
www.theatlantic.com/education/archive/2016/09/
where-sixth-graders-run-their-own-city/498257/

Wong, H. K., & Wong, R. T. (2009). *The first days of school: How to be
an effective teacher.* Mountain View, CA: Harry K. Wong.

Index

abundance-oriented approach to
    teaching, 169–89
    collaboration in, 178–82
    don't forget joy in, 188–89
    seek flow in, 170–73
    tough skin in, 174–78
    vacate on vacation in, 185–88
    welcome experts in, 182–85
academic achievement
    well-being and, 189
accolade(s)
    passions *vs.*, 169–70
accountability
    fear-based, 122, 123
    responsibility *vs.*, 122
active gallery walk, 22–24
Adler, A., 188–89
American Psychological Association's 122nd Annual Convention, 147
American students
    food insecurity among, 9
    homelessness among, 9
    push to succeed for, 6–7
American teachers
    leaving profession, xxiii
    microcredentials of, 169–70

    neglect to leave sufficient time
        for recharging during summer,
        185–88
    stress of, 124–25
    teaching approaches of, 168–70
anchor charts
    in creating calm learning environment, 50–51
Anderson, M., 138–40
Angelou, M., 76
Angry Birds, 106
anxiety(ies)
    realities *vs.*, 177
approaches to life, 168–69
assessment(s)
    custom-made, 158–60
    student responsibility related to,
        125
Association of European Economics Education conference,
    116
athletic retreat center
    Camp School at, 43
atmosphere
    calm, 47
attentiveness
    after fifteen-minute breaks, 11

autonomy, 91–127
  coplanning in, 110–14
  demand responsibility in, 121–27
  leave margin in, 98–104
  make it real in, 114–21
  Me & MyCity program in, 115–21
  offer choices in, 104–8
  plan with your students in, 108–14
  start with freedom in, 94–98

balance
  in creating calm learning environ-
    ment, 51–52
Banana Tag, 19, 25
belonging, 57–89
  banish bullying in, 82–88
  buddy up system in, 86–89
  celebrate learning in, 72–76
  cultivating personal sense of, 61
  eating lunch with students in, 63–64
  greeting students by name in,
    62–63
  home visits in, 64–66
  know each child in, 61–66
  play with your students in, 66–71
  pursue class dream in, 76–82
  recruit welfare team in, 57–61
  teachers' need for, 57–61
  in teaching, 58–59
better-trained teachers, xv
between-school competition
  absence of, xiv
binders
  notebooks vs., 126–27
bingo
  human, 70–71
Biztown, 116
book talks, 74–76
Boydston, I., 36
brain breaks. see also fifteen-minute
    breaks
  regular, 13
  scheduling of, 9–15

ways of offering, 13–15
  whole-group, 13
breathe fresh air
  in well-being, 38–42
Brookhart, S., 154–57
buddy up system
  in cultivating sense of connected-
    ness in classrooms, 86–89
  success of, 88
bullying
  banishing, 82–88
  defined, 83
  KiVa program against, 83–86
  natural play spaces in reducing,
    44
  U.S. National Academies of Sci-
    ence, Engineering, and Medicine
    on, 83
burn out, 5–6

California High School Exit Exami-
    nation, 160
calm
  sense of, 47
calm atmosphere, 47
calm learning environment, 47–55
  anchor charts in, 50–51
  mindfulness in, 52–55
  noise meter in, 51
  strike balance in, 51–52
calmness
  in Finnish schools, 33–34
calm spot, 15
Camp School, 43
  at athletic retreat center, 43
  benefits of, 77
  as bonding experience, 77
  as class dream, 76–82
  fundraising for, 94–95
Carnegie Mellon University, 33
celebrate learning
  in cultivating sense of connected-
    ness in classrooms, 72–76

challenge(s)
  journaling in dealing with, 176–78
chart(s)
  anchor, 50–51
  KWL, 113–14
child(ren)
  freedom of, 122
  know each, 61–66
  responsibilities of, 122
choice(s)
  in autonomy building, 104–8
choice time
  qualities of, 14
class dream
  as bonding experience, 77
  Camp School as, 76–82
  in cultivating sense of connected-
    ness in classrooms, 76–82
  negotiating, 78–81
  pursue, 76–82
classroom(s)
  home economics, 72–74, 120
  mindfulness in, 52–55
  opportunities for students to
    impact, 93
  responsive, 131
  simplicity of, 33–34
  woodworking, 120
classroom environment
  ways to improve, 41
classroom instruction
  rigidity in, 136
classroom walls
  simplicity of, 32–38
  students' work displayed on, 33–36
  uncluttered, 32–38
classroom windows
  open, 38–42
class time
  physical activity during, 21–22
coaching
  in developing mastery, 150–57
Coffeehouse Poetry Day, 75–76

cognitive functioning
  time in nature and, 44
collaboration
  defined, 181
  in Finnish schools, 169
  in fostering abundance-oriented
    worldview in teaching, 178–82
  as necessity, 180
collaboration over coffee
  in fostering abundance-oriented
    worldview in teaching, 178–82
commercial curricula
  embracing, 137–41
competition
  between-school, xiv
comprehensive schooling, xiv–xv
confidence
  time in nature and, 44
connection(s)
  cultivating personal, 63
coplanning
  in autonomy building, 110–14
  KWL charts in, 113–14
  methods for, 113
"crutch(es)"
  limiting use of, 127
Csikszentmihalyi, M., 172
culture of trust, 124
curriculum
  balance in, xiv
  commercial, 137–41
  students interests connected with,
    106–8
custom-made assessments, 158–60

Davis, L.C., 53
demand responsibility
  in autonomy building, 121–27
democracy
  in school, 109
Department of Computer Science and
    Engineering
  at University of Washington, 41–42

Dewey, J., 44–45

differentiated instruction, 114,
   130–31

digital skills
   OECD on, 143

discuss grades
   in developing mastery, 163–66

Ditch That Textbook, 140–41

doc cam(s), 142–44

Do Now activities, 103–4

don't forget joy, 189
   in fostering abundance-oriented
      worldview in teaching, 188–89

dream(s)
   class, 76–82 *see also* class dream

Eagle Mountain Elementary School, 12

eating lunch with students, 63–64

Economic Information Office, 116

education
   environment-based, 42–47
   special, xvi
   teacher, xv

educator(s)
   experienced and qualified, xvi

"energizers," 21–22

enjoyment
   in choice time, 14

environment(s)
   calm learning, 47–55 *see also* calm
      learning environment
   classroom, 41
   as factor in child's ability to iden-
      tify two similar words and read
      proficiently, 49
   home, 49
   learning *see* learning
      environment(s)

environment-based education, 42–47

essential material
   teaching of, 130–37

exercise equipment
   "passports" to borrow, 20–21

experienced and qualified educators,
   xvi

expert(s)
   in fostering abundance-oriented
      worldview in teaching, 182–85

external stimuli
   reducing, 34

family background
   impact on in-school learning, xvii

fear-based accountability, 122
   adverse effects of, 123

feedback
   to students, 152

fifteen-minute breaks, xxii–xxiii,
      xxvii. *see also* brain breaks
   attentiveness after, 11
   leave margin in, 100–1
   Rhea's research project on, 12
   scheduling of, 9–15
   time spent during, 4–5
   in well-being, 9–15

Finland's Independence Day celebration
   appreciation for tranquility during,
      48
   Fourth of July celebration *vs.*, 48

Finnish language
   respect for peace in, 48

*Finnish Lessons: What Can the World
   Learn from Educational Change in
   Finland*, xviii, 129, 159–60

Finnish Paralympians, 78–79

"Finnish Report Card 2014 on Physical Activity for Children and
   Youth," 17

Finnish Schools on the Move, 17–26

Finnish students
   critical elements in excellent faring
      of, xiv–xvii

first days of school
   success determined by, 66–68

first graders teaming up with sixth
   graders, 86–89

first lesson of day
  leave margin in, 102–3
Fisher, A.V., 34, 76
Flip the System: Changing Education from the Ground Up, 178–79
flow
  described, 172
  experience of, 172–73
  in fostering abundance-oriented worldview in teaching, 170–73
  superiority *vs.*, 171–72
focus
  in achieving flow, 172–73
  time in nature and, 44
food insecurity
  in American student population, 9
Fourth of July celebration
  Finland's Independence Day celebration *vs.*, 48
freedom
  in autonomy building, 94–98
  of Finnish children, 122
fresh air
  benefits of, 39–40
  breathing, 38–42
fundraising
  for Camp School, 94–95

Gardner, H., 45
get into the wild
  in well-being, 42–47
Gonzalez, A., 53
grade(s)
  discussion of, 163–66
grading system, 157–58
gratitude
  as metastrategy, 178
Greenfield, E., 76
greening of school grounds, 46
greeting students
  by name as they enter classroom, 62–63
grouping, 68

Haapaniemi Elementary School, 47, 50
happiness
  autonomy in, 91–127 *see also* autonomy
  belonging in, 57–89 *see also* belonging
  foundation for experiencing, 8–9
  ingredients of, xxix
  mastery in, 129–66 *see also* mastery
  mind-set in, 167–89 *see also* mind-set
  as precursor to success, 8
  student well-being and standardized test scores boosted by, 188–89
  well-being in, 3–55 *see also* well-being
Hargreaves, A., 179
Harvard Business School, 187
Harvard University, 45
Havu, P., 84, 85, 87–88, 119–20, 184
health
  establishing permanent mechanisms in securing and enhancing, xv–xvi
Heard, G., 76
hierarchy
  leadership, xvi
hip-hop
  in developing mastery, 148
hobby(ies)
  impact on in-school learning, xvii
home economics classroom, 72–74, 120
home environment
  as factor in child's ability to identify two similar words and read proficiently, 49
homelessness
  in American student population, 9
home visits, 64–66
homework policy, 31–32

Hopia, J., 68
"How Noise Pollution Impairs Learn-
    ing," 49
human bingo, 70–71

ice cream shop
    children running fake, 120–21
*If You're So Smart, Why Aren't You
    Happy?*, xxix
inclusiveness
    spirit of, xv
independence
    in choice time, 14
Independent Learning Week, 95, 104–6
in-school learning
    out-of-school situations impact on,
    xvi–xvii
instruction
    differentiated, 114, 130–31
    rigidity of, 136
intelligence(s)
    "naturalist," 45
    theory of multiple, 45
International Baccalaureate pro-
    grams, xviii

Jennings, P., 53–55
joulurauha, 48
journaling
    in dealing with professional chal-
    lenges, 176–78
joy
    in fostering abundance-oriented
    worldview in teaching, 188–89
    as strategy, xxviii–xxix
"Joy Factor," xxviii
Junior Achievement, 116

Kabat-Zinn, J., 53
Kahoot!, 97–98
Kalevala Comprehensive School,
    39–40, 145–46
Kalmi, P., 117

keep the peace
    in well-being, 47–55 *see also* calm
    learning environment
Khamsi, R., 83
Khazan, O., 49
Kick the Can, 69, 71
KiVa conflict resolution session, 85
KiVa meeting, 84
KiVa program, 83–86
    against bullying, 83–86
    strategy of, 84
KiVa teacher, 84
know each child
    in cultivating sense of connected-
    ness in classrooms, 61–66
knusaamista vastaan (KiVa), 83–86.
    see also KiVa
Kraus, N., 147, 148
Kukkola, J., 47
KWL charts, 113–14

language
    respect for peace in, 48
language arts lessons
    restructuring with margin, 98–104
Last Child in the Woods, 43–46
leader(s)
    school, xvi
leadership hierarchy, xvi
learner(s)
    self-directed, 93
learning
    "appearance" of, 34
    celebrating, 72–76
    in-school, xvi–xvii
    nature-based, 42–47
    noise effects on, 48–50
    project-based, 130, 131
    proving, 157–62
    "real-world" setting for, 150–57
    reflecting on, 165–66
    relaxed, 47–48
    stress-free, 47–48

"learning by doing," 150–57
learning environment(s)
    calm, 47–55 *see also* calm learning
        environment
    welcoming, low-stress, 69–70
learning space
    simplified, 32–38
learning target(s)
    defined, 154
    workshop model with, 154–57
Learning Targets, 154
learn on the move
    in well-being, 15–26
leave margin
    in autonomy building, 98–104
    fifteen-minute breaks in, 100–1
    in first lesson of day, 102–3
Lemov, D., xxviii, 103–4
"less is more," 33
lesson(s)
    length of, 16
    sitting during, 16
Levitin, D., 13
LIKES, 18
Linnanen, J., 68, 71, 144–45, 152
listening
    mindful, 53–54
loneliness
    of teachers, 58, 60
Louv, R., 43–46
lunch
    with students, 63–64
Lyubomirsky, S., 177–78

make it real
    in autonomy building, 114–21
margin
    leave, 98–104
    restructuring with, 98–104
Martinlaakso High School, 68, 163
Martti Ahtisaari Elementary School, 68
masters-degree programs
    research-based, xv

master teachers, 169
mastery, 129–66
    coaching in, 150–57
    discuss grades in, 163–66
    mine textbook in, 137–41
    music in, 145–50
    prove learning in, 157–62
    teach essential in, 130–37
    technology in, 141–45
Math Musical Minds, 148
Matriculation Examination, 159–60
Maunula Comprehensive School, 68,
    144
McCombs School
    at University of Texas at Austin,
        xxix
McGill University, 13
Me & MyCity program, 115–21
    breakdown in collaboration among
        workers in, 118
    greater economic knowledge asso-
        ciated with participation in, 117
    inspiration for, 116
    learning benefits of, 116–17
    motivation via, 117–18
    organization of, 116
    use of, 115–16
metastrategy
    gratitude as, 178
microcredentials
    of American teachers, 169–70
Miller, D., 75–76
mindful listening, 53–54
mindfulness
    in classrooms, 52–55
mindfulness exercises, 53
Mindfulness for Teachers, 53
mindful walking, 54–55
mind-set, 167–89
    collaboration in, 178–82
    don't forget joy in, 188–89
    seek flow in, 170–73
    tough skin in, 174–78

mind-set (*continued*)
   vacate on vacation in, 185–88
   welcome experts in, 182–85
Ministry of Education and Culture, 116
Moreno, A., 15, 52
morning circle, 63
Moss, C., 154–57
motivation
   Me & MyCity program in, 117–18
multiple intelligences
   theory of, 45
music
   in developing mastery, 145–50

National Center for Children in Poverty, 8
national educational policy
   agreed-upon, 116
"naturalist intelligence," 45
nature
   in reducing bullying, 44
   time in, 42–47
nature-based learning
   benefits of, 42–47
nature-deficit disorders, 43
noise
   effects on learning, 48–50
noise meter
   in creating calm learning environment, 51
Northwestern University, 147
notebooks
   binders *vs.*, 126–27
novelty
   in choice time, 14

obesity
   time in nature as buffer to, 44
obstinate
   tough skin *vs.* being, 175
OECD. *see* Organization for Economic Cooperation and Development (OECD)

offer choices
   in autonomy building, 104–8
Ogle, D., 113
open-ended, challenging questions, 160–62
open windows
   in classroom, 38–42
Oreskovich, A-M, 148–49
Organization for Economic Cooperation and Development (OECD), xii–xiii, 129
   on digital skills, 143
out-of-school situations
   impact on in-school learning, xvi–xvii
overweight
   time in nature as buffer to, 44
Overwhelmed, 13–14, 187

Paalanen, M., 117–18
Paralympians
   Finnish, 78–79
passion(s)
   accolades *vs.*, 169–70
passivity
   in free time, 16–18
"passports" to borrow exercise equipment during recess, 20–21
Pathways to the Olympics, 131–34
PBL. *see* project-based learning (PBL)
peace
   in Finnish language, 48
Pellegrini, A., 10–11
personal connections
   cultivating, 63
perustella, 158–59
Peura, P., 163–64, 166
physical activity
   during class time, 21–22
   suggestions for increasing, 24–26
physical activity levels, 17–18

physical health benefits
 of time in nature, 44
Pinsker, J., 169
PISA (Programme for International
 Student Assessment), xii, xiv,
 xxv, xxvii, xxviii, 129
plan with your students
 in autonomy building, 108–14
play with students
 in cultivating sense of connectedness in classrooms, 66–71
Pohtola, T., 68, 124–25
private schools
 absence of, xiv
productivity
 worth quantified by, 4
professional responsibility
 in Finnish schools, 121
professional trust
 in Finnish schools, 121
Programme for International Student
 Assessment (PISA), xii, xiv, xxv,
 xxvii, xxviii, 129
project-based learning (PBL), 130, 131
 defined, 131
project-based learning (PBL) units,
 131–34
prove learning
 in developing mastery, 157–62
psychological benefits
 of time in nature, 44
pulsing
 in well-being, 13–14

question(s)
 open-ended, challenging, 160–62

Raghunathan, R., xxix, 130, 168–71,
 178, 189
Räihä, M., 38–41, 43, 145–46
Reading With Meaning, 75–76
real
 making it, 114–21

reality(ies)
 anxieties *vs.*, 177
"real-world" setting
 for learning, 150–57
*Recess: Its Role in Education and Devel-
 opment*, 10
"recess activators," 19, 25
recharge after school
 in well-being, 26–32
recruit welfare team
 in cultivating sense of connectedness in classrooms, 57–61
relaxed learning, 47–48
research-based masters-degree programs, xv
responsibility(ies)
 accountability *vs.*, 122
 assessment-related, 125
 demand, 121–27
 of Finnish children, 122
 gradual release of, 94
 professional, 121
responsive classroom, 131
Ressu Comprehensive School, xviii
Rhea, D., 12
rhymäyttäminen, 68
Richardson, W., 145
rigidity
 in classroom instruction, 136
ruokarauha, 48

safety, 47
Sage Publications, 41
Sahlberg, P., xi, 116, 129, 130, 159–60
saunarauha, 48
scarcity-minded approach to teaching, 168–70
Schleicher, A., 143
school(s)
 democracy in, 109
 highest performing, 129–30
 private, xiv
 recharge after, 26–32

school boards
  in American education decision
    making, 116
school grounds
  greening of, 46
  as habitat, 45–46
school homework policy, 31–32
schooling
  comprehensive, xiv–xv
school leaders, xvi
Schulte, B., 13–14, 187
self-directed learners, 93
sense of calm, 47
Seppälä, E., 7–8
sew
  learning how to, 119–20
Shirley, D., 179
simplified learning space, 32–38
simplify space
  in well-being, 32–38
sisu, 175–76
sitting
  prolonged, 16
  suggestions for reducing amount of
    time students are, 24–26
sixth graders teaming up with first
    graders, 86–89
slower pace, 4
space
  simplification of, 32–38
special education
  structure for, xvi
spirit of inclusiveness, xv
Springsteen, B., 149
standardized test scores
  happiness in boosting, 188–89
Stanford University, 7
start with freedom
  in autonomy building, 94–98
status of teachers, 121–22
stimuli
  reduce external, 34
stress
  of American teachers, 124–25

stress-free learning, 47–48
student(s)
  American *see* American students
  circle of, 63
  feedback to, 152
  greeting by name at door, 62–63
  opportunities to impact classroom, 93
  plan with your, 108–14
  playing with, 66–71
  teachers eating lunch with, 63–64
student interests
  curriculum connection with, 106–8
Student Welfare Team, xvi, 59–61
student well-being
  happiness in, 188–89
student work
  displaying, 33–36
success
  happiness as precursor to, 8
Sudbury Valley School, 109–10
superiority
  flow *vs.*, 171–72

talk(s)
  book, 74–76
Tammelin, T., 18
teacher(s)
  American *see* American teachers
  better-trained, xv
  eating lunch with students, 63–64
  experience of belonging by, 57–61
  Finland's trust of, 122–23
  KiVa, 84
  leaving profession, xxiii
  loneliness of, 58, 60
  looking for casual, "natural" ways
    of working with fellow teachers,
    180–81
  master, 169
  pacing themselves, 29–30
  recharging for, 26–32, 185–88
  remaining with group of children
    for more than one school year,
    61–62

status of, 121–22
trust of Finnish *vs.* American,
    121–22
vacate on vacation, 185–88
teacher education, xv
teach essential
    in developing mastery, 130–37
Teach for America, 122
teaching
    abundance-oriented approach to,
        169–89 *see also* abundance-
        oriented approach to teaching
    belonging in, 58–59
    as lonely job, 58, 60
    models of, 130–31
    scarcity-minded approach to, 168–70
Teach Like a Champion 2.0, xxviii,
    103–4
team building, 68
technology
    in developing mastery, 141–45
textbook(s)
    in developing mastery, 137–41
    use of, 136
The Atlantic, 49, 53, 169
The First Days of School, 66
"the first step in a great lesson," 103–4
The Happiness Track, 7–8
The New York Times, 36
theory of multiple intelligences, 45
The School and Society, 44–45
The Well-Balanced Teacher, 138–40
time spent in nature
    in well-being, 42–47
Tomlinson, C.A., 114
tough skin
    being obstinate *vs.*, 175
    described, 176
    in fostering abundance-oriented
        worldview in teaching, 174–78
traditional testing, 157–58
tranquility
    in Finland's Independence Day
        Celebration, 48

trust
    culture of, 124
    of Finnish *vs.* American teachers,
        121–23
    professional, 121
tunnelma, 33
"turn-and-talk," 48
"2014 United States Report Card on
    Physical Activity for Children
    and Youth," 17

University of California, Riverside, 178
University of Minnesota, 10
University of Oregon, 48–49
University of Pennsylvania, 188
University of Texas at Austin
    McCombs School at, xxix
University of Vaasa, 117
University of Virginia, 114
University of Washington
    Department of Computer Science
        and Engineering at, 41–42
University of Wisconsin, 49
university teaching programs, 122
U.S. National Academies of Science,
    Engineering, and Medicine
    on bullying, 83

vacate on vacation
    in fostering abundance-oriented
        worldview in teaching, 185–88

walk(s)
    active gallery, 22–24
Walker, J., xxi–xxiv
Walker, M., 123
Walker, T., xviii, xix, 4
walking
    mindful, 54–55
wall space
    classroom, 32–38
welcome experts
    in fostering abundance-oriented
        worldview in teaching, 182–85

welcoming, low-stress learning envi-
    ronment
  fostering of, 69–70
welfare team
  in cultivating sense of connected-
    ness in classrooms, 57–61
well-being, 3–55
  academic achievement related to,
    189
  brain breaks in, 9–15
  breathe fresh air in, 38–42
  establishing permanent mecha-
    nisms in securing and enhanc-
    ing, xv–xvi
  get into the wild in, 42–47
  keep peace in, 47–55
  learn on the move in, 15–26
  pulsing in, 13–14

recharge after school in, 26–32
  simplify space in, 32–38
  strategies for promoting, 13–14
whole-group brain breaks, 13
window(s)
  open classroom, 38–42
Wong, H., 66
Wong, R., 66
woodworking classroom, 120
word identification
  home environment effects on, 49
workshop model
  with learning targets, 154–57
Worth, V., 76

Yolen, J., 76
Yrityskylä, 115–21. see also Me &
    MyCity program